'wo wee

?''

EARLY CALIFORNIA:
Perception and Reality

Papers read at a Clark Library Seminar
12 May 1979

by

Henry J. Bruman
Clement W. Meighan

William Andrews Clark Memorial Library
University of California, Los Angeles / 1981

Introduction

THE FOUR HUNDREDTH anniversary of Sir Francis Drake's five-week sojourn in California (17 June to 23 July 1579) provided many opportunities for celebration. A state commission was created by enabling legislation, California Assembly Bill 252 of 1973, to plan, coordinate, and execute various commemorative activities, particularly for the quadricentennial year, 1979. The centerpiece of the celebration was a week-long international conference, which culminated in Grace Cathedral, Nob Hill, San Francisco, on the anniversary of the landing day, 17 June, when the Right Reverend and Right Honourable Gerald A. Ellison, the Lord Bishop of London, preached the sermon at Evensong, followed by a Te Deum of thanksgiving for the discovery of California by Sir Francis Drake.

Both preceding and following this religious service were various activities—lectures, exhibitions, parades, plays, receptions—involving some of the most prestigious institutions in California: the Huntington Library, the Bancroft Library, the J. Paul Getty Museum, the California Academy of Sciences, the Museum of Man, San Diego, and the Oakland Museum, where the British Library exhibition "The Famous Voyage of Sir Francis Drake, 1577–1580" was mounted from 17 June through 8 September.

Charter Day, 5 April 1979, at the University of California honored Drake, with British ambassador to the United States, His Excellency Peter Jay, and American ambassador to the United Kingdom, His Excellency Kingman Brewster, Jr., being the featured speakers. The university also appointed Commander David W. Waters of the National Maritime Museum,

iii

Greenwich, as Regents' Professor on the UCLA campus during the spring quarter, 1979.

To the statewide Drake celebrations UCLA's William Andrews Clark Memorial Library made notable contributions. Dr. Helen M. Wallis, Map Librarian, British Library, served as the Clark Library Senior Research Fellow, April through July 1979. The 1979 six-week Summer Postdoctoral Fellowship Program at the Clark Library was on the theme "Between Drake and Cook: English Maritime Enterprise in the Seventeenth and First Half of the Eighteenth Centuries." The main title of this seminar recognizes the two greatest of British navigators—the year 1979 was the bicentennial of the death of Captain James Cook in Hawaii as well as the quadricentennial of Drake on the California coast. These two discoverers were also honored in a joint UCLA and California Academy of Sciences exhibition, "From Drake to Cook: Two Centuries of British Discovery in the Pacific."

In addition to the appointment of Helen Wallis and the six-week summer program, the Clark Library on Saturday 12 May sponsored an all-day seminar, "Early California: Perception and Reality," followed by the Clark Library Revels, a program of musical and dramatic entertainment. These events honored the native peoples of California as well as the explorers of the area—Spanish, English, Russian, and American. The date chosen for the seminar and revels was the approximate time of year when Drake would have been off the coast of southern California, albeit far out of sight of land. Drake had left Guatulco, Oaxaca, Mexico, on 16 April and returned from north of 40° N latitude to a California anchorage at about 38° N—present Marin County—in mid June.

The morning speaker at the seminar on 12 May was Professor Henry J. Bruman of the Department of Geography at the University of California, Los Angeles. Henry Bruman was born in Berlin and came to California when he was nine years old. He attended Manual Arts High School in Los Angeles and went to the California Institute of Technology on a freshman scholarship. As a sophomore he came to UCLA and was graduated in 1935 with a major in chemistry and a minor in astronomy. In 1934 he took a summer course at the National University of

Mexico, where he discovered geography. He was later influenced in this subject at UCLA by Professors Ruth E. Baugh and George McCutcheon McBride, and at Berkeley as a graduate student by Carl Sauer, receiving his Ph.D. in 1940. He taught at Pennsylvania State College (now University) until 1943, when he joined the Institute of Social Anthropology of the Smithsonian Institution and later the M (Migration) Project, where his work was on postwar refugee colonization in Brazil. In 1945 Bruman returned as a faculty member to UCLA, where he has conducted research on the culture history of tropical plants and on Alexander von Humboldt; he was chairman of the Department of Geography from 1957 to 1961 and held various appointments in the Latin American Center until 1965. He has held a field fellowship from the Social Science Research Council, a research contract and appointment as naval technician from the Office of Naval Research, a Fulbright Fellowship for work in Portuguese archives, and several contracts with the Department of State. From 1966 to 1968 Bruman was Visiting Professor of Geography and director of the University of California Study Center at Georg August University at Goettingen. He was awarded the Alexander von Humboldt Gold Medal by the Federal Republic of Germany in 1971 and the Medal of Honor by Georg August University in 1979. Professor Bruman has established a fellowship in cultural-historical geography at UCLA as well as an endowment in the UCLA Map Library.

Professor Clement W. Meighan of the Department of Anthropology at UCLA was the afternoon speaker at the 12 May seminar. Clement Meighan was born in San Francisco, where he received his early schooling. All of his college work was at the University of California, Berkeley. In 1952 Meighan received the Ph.D. from Berkeley, where he was influenced by Robert Heizer and the then recently retired Alfred Kroeber. During World War II Clement Meighan served in the United States Army in the western Pacific for four years. Upon discharge Meighan taught field archaeology at Berkeley during the period 1951–52, before joining the UCLA faculty. He was chairman of the Department of Archaeology at UCLA from 1962 to 1965 and acting director of the UCLA Center for Latin American Studies from 1965 to 1968. Professor Meighan has worked in various regional centers and at the Institute of Archaeology at UCLA. He is presently director of the UCLA Archaeological Survey. Meighan has traveled and conducted field work in many parts of the world—the Pacific, Latin America, and the Middle East. He has a long-term interest in the western United States and as early as 1949 was crew chief of excavations at Drakes Bay, where he worked intermittently until 1972. From 1969 to 1978 Meighan was a member of the State of California Historical Resources Commission, and its chairman from 1976 to 1978. He is currently adviser to the Southwest Museum. Professor Meighan's many publications reflect his varied interests but of particular relevance to his Clark seminar presentation are "Archaeological Exploration of Sixteenth-Century Indian Mounds at Drake's Bay" (coauthored with Robert F. Heizer) and "Preliminary Excavations at Thomas Site, Marin County."

The papers delivered by Professors Bruman and Meighan to a large audience were followed by the Clark Library Revels. This program began with a fanfare and madrigals. Then followed dances from the court of Queen Elizabeth and entr'acte music, selections from Diego Ortiz. Scenes from *The Indian Emperour* by John Dryden were then performed, and music and dances from the court of Queen Anne concluded the program. Many people and organizations made the program possible; these contributions are indicated on a special program printed for the occasion. Saturday 12 May 1979 was a red-letter day at the Clark Library, when entertainment and scholarship were combined in a most felicitous manner.

NORMAN J. W. THROWER
President, Sir Francis Drake Commission,
State of California, and
Professor of Geography,
University of California,
Los Angeles

I

Sovereign California: The State's Most Plausible Alternative Scenario

HENRY J. BRUMAN

SINCE LONG BEFORE the Gold Rush, California had been considered by many impressionable visitors as one of the most attractive places on earth, as a region of such superb natural endowment as to have the potential to become a second paradise. In recent years more perceptive residents have come to rue the persistence of this excessively favorable reputation, as the continuing influx of ever more people has degraded the very qualities that attracted them. But California in earlier years was undeniably wonderful, harboring some of the most benign and pleasantly habitable areas on this planet.

I would like in this paper to comment on several interrelated themes:

1. The environmental uniqueness of California in North America and the scarcity of similar areas elsewhere;
2. The late settlement of the area as compared to central Chile, the only climatic analogue in the Americas;
3. The reasons for California's deep sleep, that period of 160 years in the seventeenth and eighteenth centuries when the region, although discovered, lay completely neglected and abandoned by Europeans, to be followed by a period of unprecedented acceleration in the historic process; and finally
4. The identification of a decisive moment when California came to a strategic crossroads, and a speculative scenario of what might have happened had a royal command been obeyed.

I thank my colleagues Raymond H. Fisher and Norris C. Hundley for their helpful suggestions.

There are in the world five areas that have what geographers call a Mediterranean climate, characterized by summer drought, winter rainfall, and generally benign temperatures (fig. 1). The largest of these by far is the classical Mediterranean itself, with the climate found mostly along the fringe areas of the inland sea, but extending into the Atlantic to include Madeira and the Canaries and eastward past the Levant into Iran. The other areas are smaller: the tip of South Africa; two separated regions in southwestern and southern Australia; a small stretch of central Chile; and part of California. In every case the influence of the Mediterranean climate is extended some distance beyond its strict limits into a surrounding fringe of drier steppe country. The climatic characteristics are the consequences of the workings of atmospheric physics within specific latitudinal limits on the western sides of continents and are fairly similar in the five cases. The adaptations of plants and animals in the five areas have many parallels. But indigenous human cultures have displayed enormous differences in content and level of sophistication.

The classical Mediterranean realm is the area in which most of the roots of Western civilization are found. The history of agriculture is ancient here, and a great assemblage of plants for food and other uses has been domesticated from the native flora. Most of these native plants are cold starting, that is, they germinate in the winter and early spring, utilizing the cold season rainfall, since summers are dry. But the great age of agriculture in the region has given rise to many adjunct technologies, such as terracing and irrigation, which have greatly widened agricultural possibilities, permitting the introduction from other areas of domesticated plants that are warm starting, adapted to the utilization of warm season rainfall for germination and growth.

Of the four other areas of Mediterranean climate in the world, only central Chile had a native population of farming peoples in possession of an assemblage of domesticated plants accustomed to a regime of winter rain and summer drought. California, except for a narrow strip along the lower Colorado, was a nonagricultural area, and useful plant domesticates had never been selected and improved out of the native flora by the

4

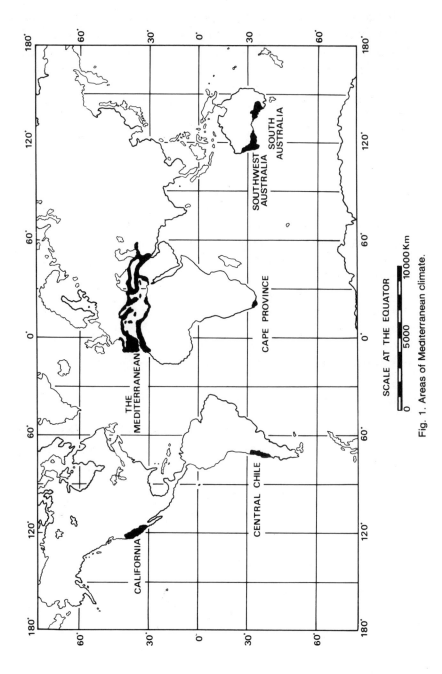

SCALE AT THE EQUATOR

0   5000   10000 Km

Fig. 1. Areas of Mediterranean climate.

Indians. This absence of locally grown native foods was to turn into a considerable disadvantage when European colonization began.[1] When the Spaniards had a first look at California through the eyes of the Cabrillo expedition in 1542, this was in every sense a primitive area of no initial attractiveness. Geographic knowledge had not yet advanced to the point where the facts of climatic symmetries on the various continents were accurately known.[2] Little did they realize, in the sixteenth century, that if there was any area in the New World that deserved the name New Spain on geographical and climatic terms, it was California and not Mexico. In fact, they might well not have cared, since their aim was not to create a new Spain but to enrich the old one (fig. 2).

One of the extraordinary contrasts between California and Chile lies in the sequence of their historic development by the Spaniards, even though their first stages were oddly similar. They were discovered about the same time, in the early 1540s, as mopping-up or supplementary operations after the conquest of the Aztecs and the Incas.[3] But the Cabrillo expedition came back having found little of interest to the Spaniards, whereas Valdivia and his successors immediately began to establish permanent settlements. Thus we have this extraordinary gap between the dates of founding of the first Spanish towns: Santiago, Chile, 1541; San Diego, California, 1769; and to pick two others in the drier country farther from the coast: Mendoza, Argentina, 1561; Riverside, California, 1870. Such a great discrepancy is really extraordinary,[4] given the similar environmental attractions of the two areas, and it deserves an explanation.

As I see it, there are basically two explanations, and they reinforce each other. The first is rooted in the obvious fact that the initial requirement from the Spanish point of view was to eliminate the independent functioning of the native states and the power of the indigenous military forces. The Incas, with their capital at Cusco in 8° S latitude, had extended their sway along the Cordillera of the Andes and along the coast north to the equator and south into central Chile. They had expanded as far south as the Río Maule, near 36° S latitude, even beyond the heart of the region of Mediterranean climate, where they encountered the belligerent Araucanians, with whom they had not

6

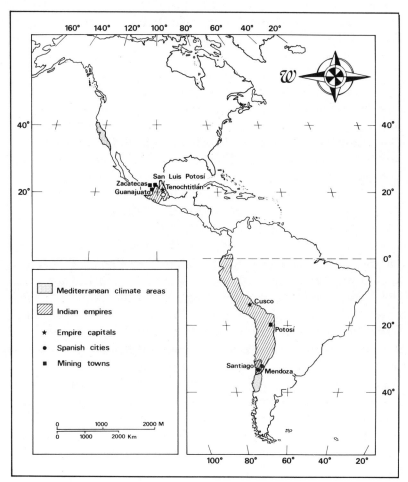

Fig. 2. Location map.

yet achieved a stable relationship when the Spaniards came. The Spaniards thus faced an unstable southern realm, *La Frontera,* just south of the Mediterranean area, and were forced to continue to devote some attention to this region for the sake of security.

In the case of the Aztecs the area dominated was smaller, more compact, and covered a lesser latitudinal spread. Whereas the Inca Empire extended over more than 4,000 kilometers north and south, the Aztecs managed barely a fourth of that. Tenochtitlán at 18° N latitude was close to the northern boundary of the empire in a rather exposed march or border site in spite of its lake, and the Aztecs had not yet been able even to take over the Tarascan state, located not far to the west of their own capital, let alone extend their control northwest along the Gulf of California or the Pacific Coast. The conquest of the Aztec state did not lead the Spaniards anywhere near California, which lay far beyond the limits of higher culture. The discovery of the "island" of (Baja) California by the men of Cortés was not so much the result of a military advance (as was the thrust into Chile by Valdivia) as it was a simple exploratory penetration into the unknown. In any event, southern Baja California is climatically more analogous to the Atacama than to California itself. This difference, then, between Chile and California in the extent of the important native states and the complementary military and governmental response of the Spaniards is one of the great reasons for the disparity in time of development between the two New World areas with Mediterranean climate.

A second reason emerges in the early colonial period. The neutralization of native military strength was followed by the confiscation of native treasure and the organization of subjugated peoples to produce and pay tribute. Next came the search for the sources of native treasure and the identification of the great silver lodes, Potosí in Peru and Zacatecas, Guanajuato, and San Luis Potosí in Mexico. Problems of providing the new mines with labor, food, work animals, and charcoal had then to be solved. In the case of Peru the main difficulties were environmental: extreme elevation, extreme aridity, and the lack of all needed supplies in the immediate area of Potosí. Supply regions were organized mainly to the south, beyond the subtropical des-

8

ert, in Mediterranean Chile and east of the Andes in what is now northwestern Argentina. Thus these southern hemisphere regions of climatic attractiveness and impressive economic potential were integrated almost at once into the main economic activity of colonial Peru, the mining, processing, and transportation of silver.

In Mexico the problem was not so much environmental as cultural. The elevations of the mines were much lower than in Peru, and climatic conditions much less rigorous. Unfortunately the mines were located mostly north of the native agricultural frontier, in lands of nomadic, nonfarming Indians. Out of necessity supply areas for the mines were established by the Spaniards in the old agricultural areas farther south. As for the area of Mediterranean climate comparable to that of central Chile, it lay in southern California, 3,000 kilometers to the northwest, unknown, not identified as the true "New Spain" from the climatic point of view, and never integrated into the mainstream of Mexican colonial activity.

THE ENGLISH

Let us now turn briefly to the Elizabethan interlude. Drake had come into the Pacific through the Strait of Magellan, being buffeted eastward afterwards near the southern tip of South America. The Spaniards at first refused to credit this, preferring to believe that he must have found the Northwest Passage. After sailing far to the north on an unsuccessful quest of this mythical strait, he turned south once more to find a place to careen and caulk his ship. This he may have found in the lee of Point Reyes, a promontory probably seen by Cabrillo but still effectively beyond the Spanish realm (figs. 3, 4, 5).

We depend for much of our information about Drake's circumnavigation on his chaplain Francis Fletcher; Fletcher's description of the winds, fog, and cold that Drake and his crew encountered along the California coast is both graphic and extensive, spreading over five pages of the printed account.[5] He speaks of "extreame and nipping cold," of "pinching cold that did benumme them," of ". . . many extreme gusts and flawes

9

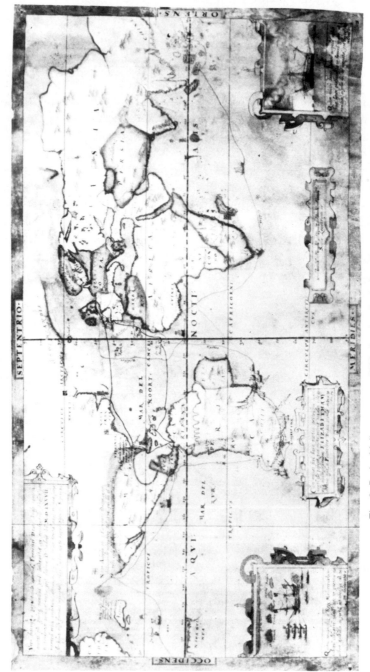

Fig. 3. Drake-Mellon map ca. 1583 showing Drake's passage around the world.

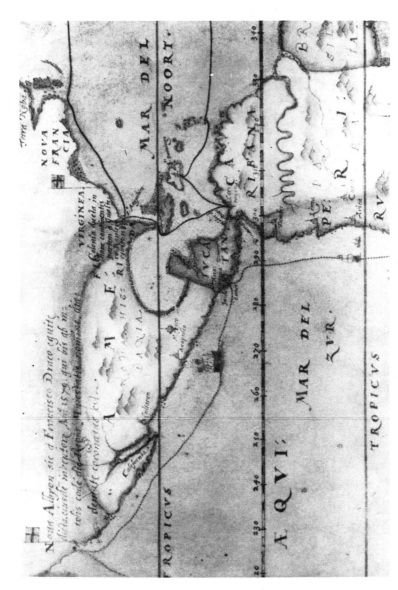

Fig. 4. Drake-Mellon map, detail, showing Drake's anchorage in California and the extent of the claim of *Nova Albion*.

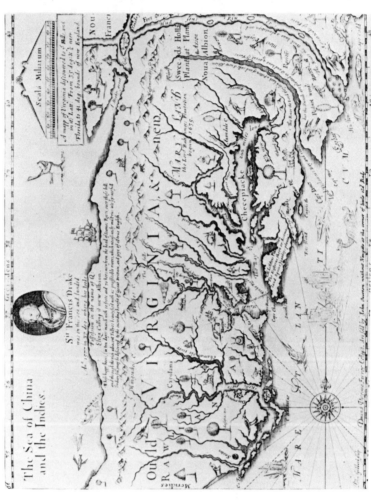

Fig. 5. Map by Virginia Farrer, ca. 1670, showing the Virginia Colony in relation to Drake's *Nova Albion*.

that beate vpon vs, which if they ceased and were still at any time, immediately upon their intermission there followed most uile, thicke, and stinking fogges, against which the sea preuailed nothing, till the gusts of wind againe remoued them. . . ." He also guesses at the causes of the low temperatures, postulating that Asia and America spread out over large areas some distance to the north, so that they nearly or quite touch. From their high and snow-covered mountains cold north and northwest winds blow out, ". . . (the constant visitants of those coasts) . . . to the infecting the whole aire with this insufferable sharpnesse: not permitting the Sunne, no, not in the pride of his heate, to dissolve that congealed matter and snow, which they haue breathed out so nigh the Sunne. . . ."[6] He even relates that the hills overlooking the coast around latitude 38° were covered with snow— in June! Now it is true that the coast north of San Francisco is commonly cold and windy in spring and early summer. Temperatures in the low fifties and high forties occur, reflecting the low temperature of the California Current. But snow on the hills in June is difficult to credit, and one wonders what to make of this statement. And this is not all. He further says: "Besides, how vnhandsome and deformed appeared the face of the earth it selfe! shewing trees without leaues, and the ground without greennes in those moneths of *June* and *July*. The poore birds and foules not daring (as we had great experience to obserue it), not daring so much as once to arise from their nests after the first egge layed, till it, with all the rest, be hatched and brought to some strength of nature, able to help itselfe. Onely this recompence hath nature affoorded them, that the heate of their owne bodies being exceeding great, it perfecteth the creature with greater expedition, and in shorter time than is to be found in many places."

It is true that in the section where he records Drake's brief foray into the interior to see the Indian settlements and "to be the better acquainted with the nature and commodities of the country," he paints a more attractive picture: "The inland we found to be farre different from the shoare, a goodly country, and fruitfull soyle, stored with many blessings fit for the vse of man. . . ." But the statement is short and does little to undo the

13

pronounced negative picture he has presented before. One thing is certain: The overall effect of his description was not one to make Nova Albion an attractive goal for future Elizabethan enterprise, even if other circumstances had permitted it. Only if there had been clear evidence of the availability of precious metals or other treasure would the virtues of New Albion (as it came to be known later) have assumed a more desirable aspect in Elizabethan minds. But there were none; the gold of the Mother Lode did not reveal itself to Drake.[7] And thus, because the qualities of New Albion were mediocre as reported, because no convenient access by way of a Northwest Passage around northern North America had been found, and because New Albion by way of southernmost South America was as far from England as any place on earth, no serious attempt was made to follow up on Drake's discovery until the coming of another age, some two centuries later, in the days of Captain James Cook and Captain George Vancouver. Instead, English efforts in the New World came to be focused on the Atlantic Coast of North America, on Virginia[8] and on the area to the north that came to be called New England, an echo of the earlier name New Albion.

SPAIN AND THE MANILA GALLEON

One consequence of the Magellan-Elcano circumnavigation of the world (1519–22) was Spain's claim to possession of the Philippine Islands. Because of prior agreements with Portugal over spheres of influence, contact with these islands could be maintained only by way of America and the Pacific. By 1570 a quasi-permanent maritime communication schedule was in operation, with Acapulco and Manila as the termini (fig. 6). This traffic, which the Spaniards called "La Nao de la China," and which we have come to know as the "Manila Galleon," continued to function, mostly on an annual basis, until the War of Independence in Mexico in the early nineteenth century.

The Manila Galleon was mainly a far-ranging commercial enterprise, profitable for some, exchanging Mexican silver for silk, porcelain, and tea from the Far East. Overall it operated at a loss, but it continued to be subsidized by the Spanish Crown,

14

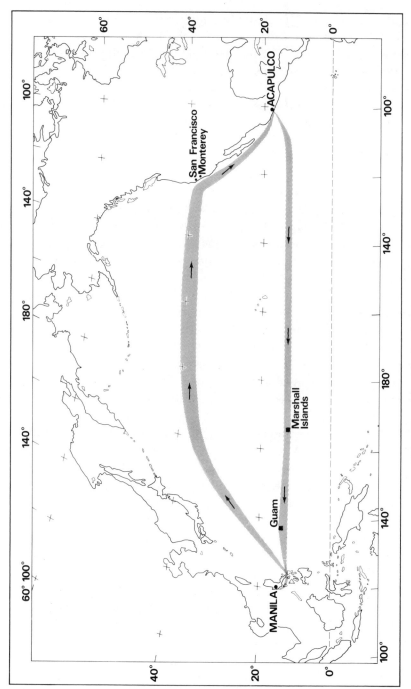

Fig. 6. Generalized tracks of the Manila Galleon.

as it was also the vehicle for the maintenance of governmental, military, and ecclesiastical affairs in the Philippines. A troublesome problem stemmed from the great length of the voyage, normally two to two and one-half months with the NE trades from Acapulco to Manila, but often four to six months and sometimes seven and even eight months by the changeable westerlies on the return. The eastward voyage was commonly so arduous that by the time the first land along the California coast was sighted provisions of all kinds were near exhaustion and the health levels of both officers and crew were dangerously undermined.[9]

The common seamen were mostly Filipinos, especially on the return voyage to Acapulco, and conditions on the galleon were so miserable that large numbers of them jumped ship and refused to make another trip across the Pacific. For example, the galleon *Espírito Santo* arrived in Acapulco in 1618 with seventy-five Filipino seamen. Only five of them made the return voyage.[10] Before the end of the sixteenth century it became evident that a reprovisioning post somewhere along the California coast, preferably near the first landfall between 42° and 37° N latitude, would be a great help to the galleon trade and a boon to the beleaguered crews. A fortified base for defense of the treasure-laden galleons against intruders in the tradition of Drake and Cavendish was also desirable, especially since it appeared to the Spaniards that the Elizabethans must have discovered the Northwest Passage and could thus prey upon north Pacific shipping at will (fig. 7).

Early in 1593 the viceroy was ordered by the Crown to institute explorations of the California coast to seek the desired haven for the returning galleons. The first response was the unfortunate voyage of Sebastián Rodríguez Cermeño, which resulted in the shipwreck of the fully laden returning galleon *San Agustín* in Drakes Bay in 1595. To the Indians it may have seemed like an extraordinary sequel to the Drake visit sixteen years earlier, although Cermeño does not mention this, but to the viceroy it was a bitter disappointment and a lesson that coastal exploration is not best carried out by crews tired at the end of lengthy and exhausting voyages. Accordingly, a new approach was tried, with an expedition sent out direct from Mexico with the sole assignment to reconnoiter the outer coast of

16

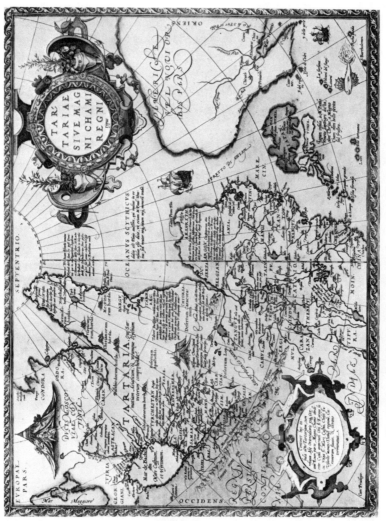

Fig. 7. Map of Tartary by Abraham Ortelius, 1584, showing a narrow
North Pacific Ocean and California firmly attached to the mainland.

California and to find the needed harbor. Assigned to command the expedition was Sebastián Vizcaíno.

The story of Vizcaíno and the California harbor for the galleons is lengthy and tortuous, and at times reads somewhat like a comedy of errors.[11] Two suitable bays were identified by Vizcaíno along the California coast in 1602, San Diego and Monterey. Monterey, first written Monterrey, and named in honor of the viceroy, Gaspar de Zúñiga y Acevedo, Conde de Monterrey, was preferred over San Diego because it lay closer to the first landfall of the galleons in the eastern Pacific. Like other navigators before and long after him, he did not discover the Golden Gate and San Francisco Bay. Through the efforts of Vizcaíno and the viceroy, who no doubt was pleased by the choice of name, assent was obtained from all appropriate authorities, and in 1606 a Royal Order was sent to Mexico spelling out in detail how the Monterey settlement was to be founded under Vizcaíno's command with supplies and settlers to be brought from the Philippines by the next galleon. Unfortunately, another viceroy was in charge in New Spain by this time, Juan de Mendoza y Luna, Marqués de Montesclaros, who was not in agreement with the plans for Monterey. Whether the fact that it was to be named after his predecessor influenced his position is not clear. Because of the great lapse of time, owing to the slowness of dispatches, it was not necessary for him to oppose the king's command directly. He merely pointed out that the ship for Manila had left a month before the Royal Order was received and that Vizcaíno had returned to Spain some months before. He further recommended that plans for developing Monterey be abandoned, and that a reprovisioning point for the galleons be established farther west, at the (mythical) islands of Rica de Oro and Rica de Plata, since by the time the ships reached California they were only twenty-five or thirty days from Acapulco. He was supported in his position by Fray Antonio de la Ascensión, who had been with Vizcaíno in California waters, and who wrote the king that Monterey Bay was insecure and that the whole plan was a scheme by Vizcaíno to gain personal wealth. Accordingly a Royal Order in 1608 suspended the Order of 1606 and ordered a search for Rica de Oro and Rica de Plata, but Monterey was to be settled in case they could not be

18

located. The two islands were of course never found, but Monterey was not settled for over 160 years. Ascensión himself advocated the settlement of Monterey in a letter to the king in 1620, but without result. Bureaucratic proceedings relative to the possible settlement of Monterey continued into the 1620s and 1630s, but came to an indecisive end. Thus, by default, Spain passed by her chance to neutralize English claims to New Albion and to settle California as a counterpoise to English settlements in Virginia and New England.[12]

And so the deep sleep began. The galleons continued to sail across the Pacific, bringing their cargoes of oriental goods, manned by scurvy-ridden, sick and dying crews. The longer the time of the voyage, the greater the cost in morbidity and mortality. Already in Vizcaíno's lifetime the efficacy of both citrus juice and palm wine as antidotes to scurvy had been published,[13] but the information was not widely disseminated and the galleon crews continued to suffer. After the establishment of Jesuit missions in Baja California the galleons, beginning in the 1740s, would sometimes stop near Cape San Lucas for succor and provisions, even though they were by then on the last leg to Acapulco.

The end of the deep sleep did not finally come until 1769, when Fray Junípero Serra and his Franciscan friars established the first of the Alta California missions at San Diego. Since the time of Vizcaíno there had been little Spanish activity in the far northwest of New Spain except for the gradual advance of the Jesuits beginning in the 1590s in Sinaloa and ending at the time of the expulsion in 1767–68 with a net of missions extending into Arizona and covering the entire peninsula of Baja California. Other nationalities had had very little contact with California, and the danger of pirates in east Pacific waters had largely disappeared by the beginning of the eighteenth century (figs. 8, 9, 10).

But then the situation changed drastically. From its long period of neglect California, and with it the entire Pacific Northwest, emerged into international prominence, and Spain was suddenly aroused out of her complacency and forced into countermoves to protect her interests. The major new political or

19

Fig. 8. Map of North America by Nicholas Sanson, 1700, showing California as an island, based on Fray Antonio de la Ascensión's false conjectures.

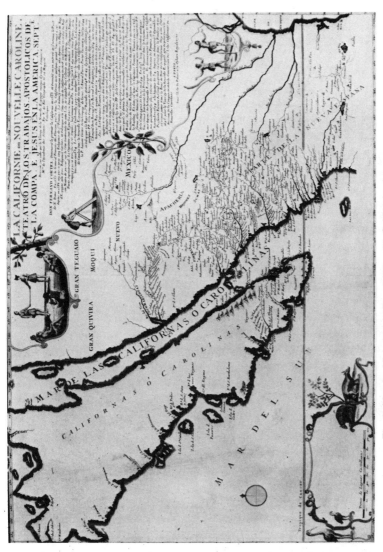

Fig. 9. Map by Nicholas de Fer, 1703, with California shown noncommittally as either an island or attached to the mainland.

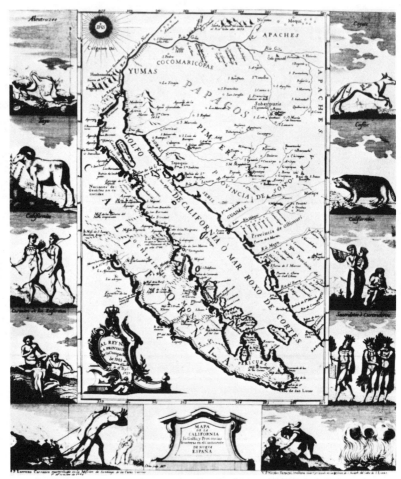

Fig. 10. Map in Miguel Venegas, *Noticia de la California* (Madrid, 1757), based on Father Kino's explorations of 1697 to 1699 as depicted on the map of Father Consag, showing Baja California as a peninsula.

quasi-political threats beginning about 1750 and continuing well into the nineteenth century included:

1. Russia's activity in Alaska and her gradual expansion toward the southwest as far as Fort Ross and Bodega Bay.
2. The scientific exploring expeditions of England, France, and Russia in the northeast Pacific.
3. The territorial claims of England from central California northward, based on New Albion, the westward expansion of the Hudson's Bay Company, and the discoveries of Captain James Cook.
4. The expansive activities of the newly independent United States, including the explorations of Lewis and Clark to the mouth of the Columbia River and the settlement of Fort Astoria to promote the hunting of sea otters.

To counteract the serious foreign threats to her interests Spain initiated three parallel programs of her own:

1. The scientific exploration of the Northwest Coast.
2. The missionization and military occupation of Alta California.
3. The exploration by land from Sonora for the support of the new settlements in California.

Although the Spaniards recognized the increasing danger to the security of their northwestern outposts in Alta California and beyond, they showed a curious residual complacency verging on blindness with respect to their colonization policy. Since the late sixteenth century the Jesuit, Dominican, and Franciscan missionaries had tried to keep secular settlers away from the neighborhood of the missions because of their disruptive influence on the lives of the Indian converts. This policy was later extended to the presidios and continued to be enforced by law to the very end of Spanish sovereignty in the nineteenth century, even though the greatest need for strategic security was a more massive Spanish presence on the land. Alexander von Humboldt quotes with approval from the diary of Dionisio Galiano:

> It is really distressing that military men, who have a hard and difficult life, cannot settle down in the country in their old age and devote themselves to farming. This regulation against building [private] houses near the presidio is against all the dic-

23

tates of common sense. If whites were allowed to engage in the tillage of the soil and the raising of livestock; if military men, by settling their wives and children on individual farms, could prepare a haven for themselves against the need to which they are only too often subject in their old age, New California would in a short time become a flourishing colony, a port of infinite usefulness to Spanish seamen who trade with Peru, Mexico, and the Philippine Islands.

He adds his own comment:

If the obstacles we have just mentioned were removed . . . the shores of San Francisco and Monterey would be settled by a large number of whites. But what a striking contrast [there is] between the colonization policies observed by the Spaniards and those through which Great Britain has in a few years created villages on the east coast of New Holland [Australia].[14]

THE RUSSIAN CHALLENGE

The only foreign penetration of California in Spanish times that threatened to carve out a permanent fief for a foreign state was that of the Russian American Company. It was a brief but intense challenge that was limited mainly by the aftereffects of the Napoleonic wars and the low reproduction rate of the sea otter.

By 1750 the Russians had discovered the riches in otter skins that could be obtained in the Aleutian Islands with the help of Aleut natives. Initially it was a plentiful resource with a ready market in the internal Russian trade as well as in China. A limiting factor gradually became evident in the slow rate of reproduction of the sea otter, a pair rarely producing more than one pup a year. The rapidly growing market for the attractive skins brought about a decimation of otters in the Aleutians between 1770 and 1780 and a need to shift the main hunting grounds farther east and south along the Gulf of Alaska. Founded in 1799, New Archangel (Sitka) became in 1808 the headquarters of Russian activity, and Aleuts were brought to the new frontier because of the unsuitability of the local Indians. Here too a prompt decline in the otter occurred, and even further advances down the coast became necessary.

The need for a supplementary food supply led first to a contact with the San Francisco Presidio in 1805, whence wheat supplies were obtained on an increasingly reliable basis well into the Mexican period, and second to the founding of Russian California at Fort Ross and Bodega Bay on lands claimed but not settled by Spain. The contrast between the rigors of Alaska and the benign plenty of California made a profound impression on the Russians, as did the evident weakness of the Spanish hold on the area. Numerous were the recommendations to the tsar that at least part of California be acquired for Russia. It was thought of mainly as a food supply base for the northern otter hunting grounds, but in at least one case the suggestion was made that families of peasants be introduced from European Russia[15] (fig. 11).

The most serious efforts came in the aftermath of the Napoleonic wars, when Spain's hold on her American empire was crumbling. The wars of Latin American independence were under way and the Monroe Doctrine had not yet been pronounced. A contemporary dispatch in the *Neue Geographische Ephemeriden* from a Washington correspondent, here retranslated, gives an insight into the rumored negotiations:

Concerning the Cession of California to Russia

Washington, November 18 (1819). Our newspapers recently reported that the Russians would acquire land in California. They limited themselves to reporting the news and to expressing their amazement, no doubt because they did not know the background. Although the affair is still covered with a thick veil of secrecy, it is not really so secret that one could not see through it. In the confidential circles of our statesmen the following rumor is making the rounds. At the Congress of Vienna the former Spanish Minister Pizarro had several private meetings with Tsar Alexander, in which the California question was decided in secret. The reason for not sharing the news of this agreement with the Congress [of Vienna] was mainly the fear that the English Ministers would express their opposition. Nevertheless, the latter suspected soon enough that a secret understanding had been reached between Russia and Spain. But these were only suspicions which were not transformed into certainties until the Russian fleet set sail for Cadiz. The British Cabinet repeatedly and with emphasis demanded an explana-

25

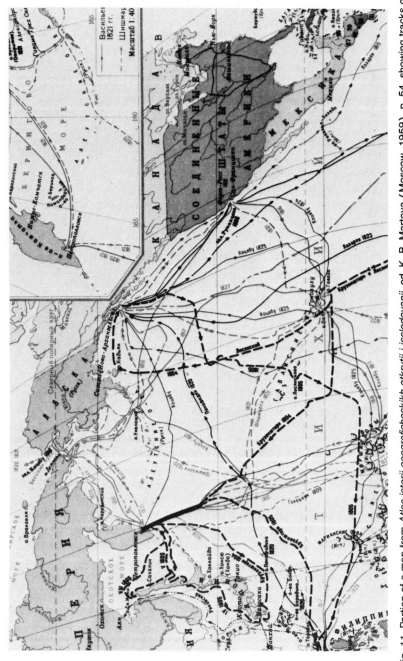

Fig. 11. Portion of a map from *Atlas istorii geograficheskikh otkrytii i issledovanii*, ed. K. B. Martova (Moscow, 1959), p. 54, showing tracks of Russian explorers and trade routes and the location of Sitka, Fort Ross, and San Francisco on the coast of North America.

tion from the Spanish Government, which was finally compelled to admit that an agreement had been reached whereby Spain would cede a considerable portion of California to Russia. The English Government protested vigorously and declared that a consummation of the agreement would be considered a hostile act. This threat caused the dismissal of Minister Pizarro. From this point on there was disagreement between the Ministers of England and Russia in Madrid. It appears that Spain, in addition to dismissing Pizarro, has promised the English Minister that the offensive agreement would be canceled. Since then, as far as can be seen, there has been no more talk of it. If, however, the facts mentioned in the papers are true, as is largely believed, one must assume either that Spain and Russia would honor the agreement, even against England, or that the latter had finally consented, since everything indicates that England, instead of following her threat to begin hostilities against Spain, will instead support her in the fight which she will probably have to face with us [the United States] in respect to the Floridas.[16]

Such a cession of part or all of Alta California to Russia in exchange for goods or military assistance could have seemed attractive to Spain as a means of salvaging at least something from an otherwise hopeless situation, but it did not materialize. In 1822 the rumor was still current, this time in the form that Tsar Alexander I would help Ferdinand VII to regain his lost American colonies in exchange for California.

The establishment of Mexican sovereignty in 1822 brought profound changes to California. Large-scale clandestine trade, which had been carried on for a generation, was now legalized, and the ports were opened to foreign shipping. Foreigners were permitted to settle down and buy land. The role of the missionaries was reduced. In 1833 the missions and all their lands were taken over by the Mexican government and were largely secularized and in part sold to private individuals by 1840. The near extinction of the sea otter and the continuing inadequacy of Russian California as a base of supplies finally persuaded the Russians to relinquish their California holdings (1841)[17] and retreat to Alaska, where they were to stay another generation before quitting America for good (1867). As more foreigners came into California, especially Yankees from the Eastern Seaboard, a quickening of economic and political life occurred and events from other parts of the continent began to exert increasing influence. When, in 1846, the war between Mexico and the United States began, California quickly became a focus of prime importance.

Texas had been broken away from Mexico by Yankee activity a decade earlier, and it set the pattern for what was to happen in California. One of the problems was how to lay claim to the Rocky Mountains and to the "Great American Desert" that lay between the Great Plains of the Louisiana Territory and the sought-after Pacific Coast. Here, from the Mexican point of view, the ingenuity and ruthlessness of the Yankee reached great heights by reducing the whole problem to one of perceptions and nomenclature. At the Treaty of Guadalupe Hidalgo in 1848 the American party produced a map of Mexico which had been made in Philadelphia the previous year (fig. 12) in which the name Alta California was spread over all of northwestern Mexico, over precisely the lands the United States wished to annex.[18] Never before had California, as perceived by Mexico, included parts of New Mexico, or the lands later to be made into Colorado, Utah, Nevada, and Arizona. But the much younger Mexican nation was defeated and disheartened by the all too evident military superiority of the United States, and thus manifest destiny was served. In one stroke Mexico gave up nearly half her territory, finally admitting that Texas was lost, and signing over all the northwestern interior as well as the crown jewel, California. In retrospect, Spain had done very little with California in her more than two and a half centuries of possession, and Mexico had had neither time nor opportunity to do much in her twenty-five years of control. The greatest irony of all was that California's gold, except for minor placers, lay undiscovered throughout the Spanish and Mexican periods, and then, in the same year as the treaty with the United States, 1848, there occurred that famous find at Sutter's Mill. As a result California became one of the most glamorous places in the world, and the rest is history. Statehood followed in two years.

Fig. 12. Map by John Disturnell, 1847, setting forth claims of the United States at the Treaty of Guadalupe Hidalgo. Note the American claim that Alta California extends eastwards to the Rocky Mountains (see note 18). This extravagant claim is reminiscent of that of the English for *Nova Albion* on the Drake-Mellon map (fig.4), where the claim extends all the way across the continent to Florida.

I would now like to point to a crucial juncture in the history of California, when a small change in policy, a different perception of opportunity, might have made an extraordinary difference in future events. I realize that with the benefit of hindsight one could easily enumerate dozens, or hundreds, of possible modifications of history that would have had important consequences, but there is a really dramatic one in California's past that deserves another look.[19] I will leave out any speculations about alternative scenarios where the geographic or historic facts make them obviously untenable. There were, for example, no Golden Cities of Cíbola for Cabrillo to discover on the California coast, and so the possibility of an early major thrust by the Spanish to conquer another rich empire was never a real one. Similarly, alas, geographic reality vetoed the early role of England in New Albion. A usable Northwest Passage did not exist, and continued access by sea in the sixteenth and seventeenth centuries was not really feasible for England in either direction around the earth. Nor did the early hope materialize that New Albion might be just a few days' march west of Virginia (fig. 5). The size of the earth, the disposition of the lands and the seas, and the location of New Albion with respect to England were all factors that, in combination with historical circumstances, dictated a delay of two centuries before England could again play a role along the Northwest Coast.

But what of Vizcaíno and his plans for a harbor in California to aid the returning Manila Galleon? Vizcaíno's proposal was accepted by the Audiencia de Mexico, the viceroy, the Council of the Indies, and the king, and the Royal Order came that the plan be carried out. Only the glacial slowness of the dispatches, the replacement of the viceroy by another less well disposed to the plan, and the reassignment of Vizcaíno before the Royal Order arrived kept it from being carried out in 1608. It was a near miss. What if it had been implemented? How might the future course of California events have been altered. I am inclined to believe that the probability at the time of the successful establishment of a Spanish settlement at Monterey was greater than the probability that it would not happen. Its not happening was

30

a direct contravention of the royal command. Funds for the settlement were made available in the decree, supplies were to be provided in the Philippines to be transported to Monterey Bay on the returning galleon, and Vizcaíno was to have full authority over the choice of settlers and over the details of site. As a reprovisioning depot for returning Manila ships Monterey would have been called upon to furnish mainly fresh water, animals for slaughter on board, and a new supply of staples such as corn, wheat, and dried beans. Fresh fruits, olive oil, and wine would have been highly prized. Other ship's stores might be required for vessels damaged en route and limited repair facilities might be desirable, but always the need was to get the merchandise as rapidly as possible to its destination in Acapulco and Puebla. Limited ranching and animal husbandry were required, and a certain amount of farming was essential. The California Indians knew nothing about raising crops. Depending on how quickly they could be pacified, their first usefulness would probably be more in helping with the animals than in working the soil. For tillage Filipinos would be mainly employed, with a leavening of Spaniards to teach irrigation agriculture in the Mediterranean manner.

What is most intriguing is what might have happened next, and what would certainly have happened after a little more familiarity with the area had been acquired: the discovery of San Francisco Bay. From the site of Monterey the nearest hilltop from which the southern end of San Francisco Bay can be seen is only fifty miles away, and from the northern end of Monterey Bay to the same place is only about twenty miles. Knowing what we know about how rapidly the Spaniards were reconnoitering in Nueva Vizcaya at this time, it is not credible to delay the probable discovery of San Francisco Bay for more than a few years after the founding of Monterey in 1608, the year of Vizcaíno's scheduled return from the Philippines with a party of settlers.

A settlement would then have been put on San Francisco Bay which would in a short time have become the main Spanish strong point in California, undoubtedly replacing Monterey as the California way station of the galleon traffic. No doubt it would have been raided by foreign ships, but in classical military terms San Francisco Bay is one of the strongest natural sites in the world, and cross fire across the Golden Gate would have been effective even in the early seventeenth century. No doubt Spanish forts would have been placed on both sides of the narrows, as well as on Alcatraz Island.

Had this scenario materialized Spain would have had a head start in California by 160 years. The settlement would have been made in the full flower of Spanish vigor and wealth. In possession of perhaps the finest natural harbor in the world, Spain would have strengthened it and populated its shores. The main thrust would have been secular, with some establishment of missions in peripheral areas. Permanent contact by land with the rest of New Spain would have had to wait a century or more. It would have been an isolated settlement, supported by sea, and more from the Philippines than from Mexico.

Miners were very active already in the mountains of north-central Mexico, and some of the more enterprising might have been tempted to try their luck in the new land to the north. Exploration by ship would have been relatively easy up San Pablo Bay, Carquinez Strait, Suisun Bay, and the Sacramento River, just as it was two hundred years later.[20] A major gold strike could conceivably have been made. The Mother Lode itself might have been turned up before the end of the seventeenth century. We know it was there, and we know the miners would have looked. Had it been found, such a strike in the seventeenth century would not have set off a vast international gold rush as it actually did in the mid-nineteenth. It would have been perceived as another of the great Spanish bonanzas in the tradition of Potosí and Zacatecas, but gold this time, not silver.[21] Thousands of people from Spain, New Spain, and the Philippines would have been attracted to the mines, and a Spanish-Mestizo-Filipino combination would have created a new and distinctive racial type in California. Cities would have grown in time around the mines and around the harbor, and a separate Audiencia de California would have had to be established.

Of course, the deeper we look into the crystal ball, the dimmer the image gets, and I am conscious of the old adage that fools step in where angels fear to tread. I don't know how to appraise what the Russians might have done around Bodega and Fort

32

Ross with such a powerful Spanish presence on the Bay. Most likely they would not have hunted otter on the Bay, and they probably would not have put in semipermanent installations. Nor do I know how to appraise this larger and better-defended Spanish colony with respect to independence, local autonomy, American penetrations, or a Mexican War.

The actual population of California shortly after the time of independence from Spain was not much more than 20,000.[22] Some thousands of these were Indians; less than a hundred were priests or monks. Even by the 1840s the effective civilian population consisted of no more than a thousand or fifteen hundred families, of which only a few dozen were big landowners. Such a sparse group, dependent on their own limited military strength except for a handful of undermanned presidios, and already containing some dozens of Yankee sons-in-law, were no match for the military forces of the United States.

I am postulating in my scenario, given 160 years longer and much greater local production of wealth, a population in California of 300,000 to 500,000 at the time of independence from Spain, among whom would be 15,000 to 20,000 civilian *Californio* families widely distributed over the central and southern part of the area of the present state. They would have been fully capable of raising their own armies and perhaps of providing them with locally manufactured arms and munitions. They could, in fact, have acted as a considerable counterpoise to English and American strength along the Atlantic Coast. One is entitled to wonder whether the ambitious young sons-in-law or the forces of the United States in the first half of the nineteenth century would have been able to take over; whether, in fact, a take-over attempt would have been made. The crystal ball gets dark, but I think there is the likelihood that California today would be an independent Latin American republic and that the lands of the contiguous United States on the Pacific would be confined largely to the former Oregon Territory.

Perhaps the moral of all this is that we should leave history well enough alone. If my scenario had materialized, we today in this spot would be in another country.

Notes

1. Even today, when California has become the leading agricultural state in the United States, not a single crop native to the area plays a significant role in commercial production, either in California or anywhere else. Of course, timber trees, such as Douglas fir, which are grown on tree "farms" are excluded.

2. The formulation of a rational climatic classification and the delineation of generalized climatic distributions on an idealized continent had to wait until the late nineteenth and early twentieth centuries. The first explicit mention, to my knowledge, of the climatic similarities among California, central Chile, and southern France, and of analogous agricultural potential, was made by the great French explorer Lapérouse, who spent part of September 1786 in the Monterey area. His insight into the geographic relationships was given a material dimension when he gave the mission fathers at Carmel some potatoes he had brought from Chile. He felt they would do well in the light, rich soils around Monterey, and that this was perhaps not the least significant present he left behind. (Jean-François de Galaup de Lapérouse, *Voyage de Lapérouse autour du monde pendant les années 1785, 1786, 1787, et 1788* [Paris: Club des libraires de France, 1965], pp. 161–63, 176.)

3. I am confining my considerations to Alta or Nueva California. The conquest of central Chile was assigned to Pedro de Valdivia, one of the lieutenants of Francisco Pizarro. It was an operation to secure the southernmost outpost of the Inca Empire and to contain the Araucanians. The reconnaissance of the California coast had originally been planned by Pedro de Alvarado, one of the lieutenants of Hernan Cortés, in the hope of finding fame and treasure in Cíbola or Quivira. When Alvarado, already in his mid-fifties, died in the Mixton War in 1541, his ships were entrusted to his younger lieutenant Juan Rodríguez Cabrillo (a navigator of Portuguese birth then working for Spain) by the viceroy Mendoza, to be used for an exploring expedition up the California coast.

4. Only one other case of delayed development of a Mediterranean area comes to mind, that of south Australia, first seen by Europeans in the early seventeenth century and not settled until toward the end of the eighteenth. But the delay in this case was only about half as long, and discovery and ultimate settlement were carried on by different maritime powers.

35

5. W. S. W. Vaux, ed., *The World Encompassed by Sir Francis Drake*, The Hakluyt Society, 1st ser., no. 16 (London, 1854).

6. His idea that Asia and America come close together farther north was a felicitous guess, since no European had yet seen Bering Strait. There is also at least a partial understanding that large land areas in high latitudes tend to be colder than adjacent water areas. The theory that lowlands near snow-covered uplands and mountains would be colder than other lowlands because of their proximity to the snow and ice held on well into the nineteenth century.

7. There is mention of treasure in the famous statement where Drake takes possession of the land in the name of the queen: "Wherefore, in the name and to the vse of her most excellent maiesty, he tooke the scepter, crowne, and dignity of the sayd countrie into his hand; wishing nothing more than that it had layen so fitly for her maiesty to enioy, as it was now her proper owne, and that the riches and treasures thereof (wherewith in the vpland countries it abounds) might with as great conueniency be transported, to the enriching of her kingdome here at home, as it is in plenty to be attained there...." A variant account printed by Hakluyt even interpolates this sentence: "There is no part of earth here to bee taken up, wherein there is not some speciall likelihood of gold or silver...." But there is nothing in the accounts to lead us to believe that Drake saw substantial "riches and treasures" among the Coast Miwok, or any evidence of the presence of gold or silver. The statements must be considered window dressing or wishful extensions to New Albion of mineral wealth known to exist many degrees farther south in the Spanish realms. It must be admitted that California had not disclosed many of its potential attractions to Drake. The benign Mediterranean climate of which we have made much was not manifest in the "most uile, thicke, and stinking fogges" and the frigid winds that belabored Drake and his crew. The low coastal growth and wind-sheared shrubs around Point Reyes gave little promise of fertile tree-covered valleys in the interior. It is doubtful if Drake or any of his men ever saw a sequoia. And the Indians he encountered were not impressive. They looked like savages, and that is precisely what they were from the point of view of the Elizabethans. They had no wealth that was recognizable as such in European eyes—no gold, no pearls, no precious stones. Had gold been a trade item between the Coast Miwok and the inhabitants of the future Mother Lode, Drake's and England's appraisal of New Albion would have been more enthusiastic and efforts to maintain contact and possession might well have been more emphatic even in the absence of a Northwest Passage.

8. "*Virginia-Britania*, is a Country in America; that lyeth betweene the degrees of 30. and 44. of the north latitude: ... as for the West thereof the Limitts are vnknowne, only yt is supposed there may be found the Discent into the South-Sea ... and sure much about the height of our Bay, *Sir Francis Drake* his *Noua Albion* ... is well conceyved to be, on the west-syde of vs, within that supposed South-Sea...."

"It is a spatious, and ample Tract of Land, from North to South, vpon a right lyne, yt may be 700. myles: from East to west in the narrowest place, supposed some 300. myles, and in other places 1000. . . ." (William Strachey, *The Historie of Travell into Virginia Britania (1612)*, ed. Louis B. Wright and Virginia Freund, The Hakluyt Society, 2d ser., no. 103 [London, 1953], pp. 31-32.)

9. For a further discussion see Henry J. Bruman, "Early Coconut Culture in Western Mexico," *Hispanic American Historical Review* 25, no. 2 (1945): 212-23.

10. To escape punishment they frequently went to remote areas in Mexico and sometimes joined Indian tribes. It was by escaped Filipino sailors that the manufacture of distilled liquors was introduced into Huichol culture and that the use of palm wine was brought to the Colima coast. (Cf. Henry J. Bruman, "The Asiatic Origin of the Huichol Still," *Geographical Review* 34, no. 3 [1944]: 418-27.)

11. The tale is developed at length, utilizing the relevant documents, in W. Michael Mathes, *Vizcaino and Spanish Expansion in the Pacific Ocean, 1580-1630* (San Francisco: California Historical Society, 1968).

12. Alexander von Humboldt, whose relationship to British scholarship was at times rather cool, and who in his diplomatic duties for the king of Prussia sometimes saw cause to distrust British political motives, takes the position that Drake and England had at best only a weak claim to New Albion between 38° and 43° N, since that coast had been discovered by Cabrillo and Ferrelo for Spain more than a generation earlier. The most England could claim by right of discovery based on Drake's voyage was the strip from 43° to 48° N. "D'après des données historiques certaines, la dénomination de *Nouvelle-Albion* devroit être restreinte à la partie de la côte qui s'étend depuis les 43° aux 48°. . . ." (Alexander von Humboldt, *Essai politique sur le royaume de la Nouvelle-Espagne*, 8° ed. [Paris: F. Schoell, 1811], 2:437.) The contrary English position is discussed in John T. Juricek, "English Territorial Claims in North America under Elizabeth and the Early Stuarts," *Terrae Incognitae* 7 (1976): 7-22. Humboldt's point of view is fully supported by the German historian Georg Friederici, whose great work on the discovery and conquest of America has not been fully appreciated by non-German scholars. In fact the latter declares that Spain's accomplishment in discovering and to a degree settling the coasts from Florida around the Gulf of Mexico and the Caribbean, again from south of Brazil to the tip of South America, and on the Pacific with but minor exceptions the entire stretch from farthest south to 55° N represents in its totality the greatest geographical accomplishment in scope, content, and significance for world history that any people on earth can point to. (Georg Friederici, *Der Charakter der Entdeckung und Eroberung Amerikas durch die Europäer*, 3 vols. [1925-36; reprint ed., Osnabrück: Otto Zeller, 1969], 1:347-56.) He is actually conservative in setting the limit at 55° N. There is

evidence in the log of navigation that the schooner *Sonora* under the command of Juan Francisco de la Bodega y Quadra reached almost 58° on 22 August 1775, more than a year before Cook on his third expedition reached these and higher latitudes. (*Colección de diarios y relaciones para la historia de los viajes y descubrimientos* [Madrid: Instituto Histórico de Marina, 1943], 2: 102–33 +, Table for August 1775 and Lámina 4.)

13. Bartolomé Leonardo de Argensola, *Conqvista de las Islas Malvcas* (Madrid, 1609), p. 9: "[Las Malucas] son agradables a la vista, pero no sanas, y menos para los estraños, todos los quales estan sugetos a la enfermedad Berber, comun en aquella tierra. Hincha los cuerpos, inhabilita los miembros; pero con el clauo y vino de las Filipinas beuido con gingibre, ò con el vso de cierta yerua, conocida de los naturales, se preseruā, y se curā; y los Holādeses cō çumo de limones, remedio hallado por el temor, y por la experiencia."

14. Humboldt, *Essai politique*, 2:449–50 (my translation). Galiano, a former officer of Malaspina, was captain of the schooner *Sutil* which along with the *Mexicana* explored the north Pacific in 1792 and accomplished the first circumnavigation of Vancouver Island.

15. Three of the more useful recent items for a study of the Russian presence in California are: James R. Gibson, *Imperial Russia in Frontier America: The Changing Geography of Russian America, 1784–1867* (New York: Oxford University Press, 1976); Kyrill T. Khlebnikov, *Colonial Russian America: Kyrill T. Khlebnikov's Reports, 1817–1832*, trans. Basil Dmytryshyn and E. A. P. Crownhart-Vaughan (Portland, Oreg.: Oregon Historical Society, 1976); and Gottfried Pfeifer, "Frontera del Norte Kaliforniens, 1800–1846: Russen, Spanier, und Angelsachsen," *Tübinger Geographische Studien*, Heft 34, Sonderband 3 (1970), pp. 255–78.

16. "Über die Abtretung Californiens an Russland," *Neue Geographische Ephemeriden*, vol. 6, no. 4 (Weimar, 1819), pp. 476–77. I do not wish to make too much of this episode because the degree of reality behind these rumors appears to be uncertain even now. It may be that historians have not yet studied the relevant archival materials. However, in the same year the following prescient comment appears in a book devoted to the new lands along the Ohio and Mississippi rivers: "We think it will not be romantic to predict that the period is not far distant, when the United States and the potent empire of Russia will be the two great master nations of the world. If the extensive coast of California be ceded to the latter, we may, perhaps, without being taken for maniacs, hazard an opinion, that the people of this western region will eventually be compelled to defend themselves against the encroachments of that gigantic power. Should this event happen after a disunion, how bitterly would posterity curse those progenitors who effected it! But we will not anticipate so disastrous an event." (Edmund Dana, *Geographical Sketches on the Western Country: Designed for Emigrants and Settlers* [Cincinnati: Looker, Reynolds & Co., 1819], p. 62.)

17. A last effort was made by Governor Wrangell in the 1830s to acquire lands for the company in the area north of the bay and west of the Sacramento River, but the best lands near the San Rafael and Sonoma missions were being rapidly converted into ranchos and sold by Mexican authorities, in part to forestall Russian designs. When Wrangell failed, the company decided to abandon California.

18. The American claim extending California to the Rockies appears to have been more the result of an innocent cartographic error committed some years earlier in England than a tactical psychological pressure play. In the late 1830s the English cartographer John Arrowsmith prepared a map to accompany the rare first edition of Alexander Forbes's *California: A History of Upper and Lower California from Their First Discovery to the Present Time* (London: Smith, Elder & Co., 1839). This map, entitled "The Coasts of Guatimala and Mexico from Panama to Cape Mendocino with the Principal Harbours of California. 1839," shows Upper or New California extending eastward through the entire drainage basin of the Colorado River to the continental divide, including even some areas south of the Gila River that had been part of Sonora for two hundred years. According to the preface, Alexander Forbes remained in Mexico while his brother John saw the manuscript through the press. Thus the map was undoubtedly prepared and published without revision by the author.

Where did Arrowsmith get his notion about the longitudinal extent of California? There appear to be no precedents for his version, either in Spanish or Jesuit maps or in those of Alexander von Humboldt, many of which would have been available to him at the Royal Geographical Society. The answer may lie in an ambiguity in the Forbes text itself. In part 2, chapter 3, Forbes says:

The part of Upper California at present occupied by the missions and settlers, is about five hundred English miles in length, and the breadth from the sea to the first range of hills may be stated at an average of forty miles, which will give an area of twenty thousand square miles and about thirteen millions of English statute acres. This however is but a small part of Upper California, as the whole country extending to the Rio Colorado, and to an undefined limit northward, is included in its territory. . . . The whole extent of Upper California properly so called presents a superficies equal to many of the most extensive and powerful kingdoms of Europe.

Such a statement, in the absence of more specific data, could perhaps be given cartographic expression in the expansive way Arrowsmith adopted, although Forbes does not say that California extends to the Colorado along it entire length, let alone that it includes the whole drainage basin, and it is clear from the text that he is getting most of his topographic information from the journal of the Garcés expedition of 1775, which traversed the region between Sonora and southern California. When he takes

39

California all the way to the Colorado River, he is referring to southern California only.

But Arrowsmith's published map was to have a strong influence on conceptions of California in the United States in the 1840s. The idea that California began at the Rocky Mountains fitted well into the contemporary geopolitical thrust of the young republic. John C. Fremont accepts the name California for the country west of the continental divide in his *Report of the Exploring Expedition to the Rocky Mountains in the Year 1842, and to Oregon and North California in the Years 1843–'44* (Washington, 1845). Perhaps following his lead, perhaps relying directly on the Arrowsmith map, several United States map makers in the early and mid-1840s adopt this usage. They are listed and discussed in Carl I. Wheat, *Mapping the Transmississippi West, 1540–1861*, 5 vols. in 6 (San Francisco: Institute of Historical Cartography, 1957–63), 2:179–84, 3:35–37, 81–87.

On the fine map of Oregon and Upper California drawn by Charles Preuss to accompany Fremont's *Geographical Memoir upon Upper California, in Illustration of His Map of Oregon and California* (Washington, 1848), California is shown extending eastward almost to the Rio Grande (called Rio del Norte). In the *Memoir* itself Fremont divides California into the Great Basin, the Sierra Nevada, and the "Maritime Region West of the Sierra Nevada," adding the telling remark (p. 12) that the latter is "the only part to which the name applies in the current language of the country."

That comment makes explicit that the extension of the name California to lands east of the Sierra rests on a conceptual error. And yet, the fact that the term was commonly so used in the 1840s by educated Americans exonerates them from potential charges of perfidy in their reliance on the Disturnell map at the Treaty of Guadalupe Hidalgo.

I thank my friend Neal Harlow for expanding my knowledge of the cartographic literature on California in the 1830s and '40s. This note is a direct result of his generous suggestion, although responsibility for the conclusions is mine alone.

19. I know many historians frown on this sort of thing as not being scholarly, and they may well be right. But in the hospitable halls of the Clark Library, where Clio, the Muse of History, must share her place on a basis of equality with the other eight, perhaps I can be forgiven.

20. Sailing ships in the seventeenth century should have had no great difficulty traversing the major channels of the delta or penetrating the lower Sacramento, just as they did not in South America when ascending the Paraná to Asunción.

21. The ancient rule of thumb among Spanish miners, coming straight out of astrology, that silver is the metal of the moon and to be found in high, cold places, whereas gold is the metal of the sun, to be found in low, hot places, would have been corroborated once again.

22. I am not including in this estimate the "wild" Indians in the remoter parts of the present state, but I do include the Indian population in the effective part of Spanish/Mexican California, which, as Humboldt points out, was essentially a coastal strip from San Diego to San Francisco with a width of about ten leagues.

II

"This Is the Way the World Ends": Native Responses to the Age of Exploration in California

CLEMENT W. MEIGHAN

This is the way the world ends
Not with a bang but a whimper.

T. S. Eliot

I WONDER WHETHER any of the coastal Indians of California, seeing the arrival of sixteenth-century Spanish and English ships, realized that the world of the Indians was over, and that with the coming of the Europeans the Indian culture was fated to disappear. Probably not, since clairvoyance was no more common with Indians than with Europeans. Yet the coming of Cabrillo, Drake, Cermeño, and their successors was not only to result in changes of political and economic kinds, but to eliminate the whole perception of the world as the Indians knew it, and to make obsolete a way of life that had functioned for thousands of years. Although it was to be centuries before the impacts of European discovery were to be fully realized, the coming of the Europeans was truly the end of the world for the native populations.

There were no particular fireworks in the initial contacts between Europeans and the native people of California—no war of conquest, no establishment of the dominion of one power over another (except in ceremonial land claims), and no plundering of a newly conquered land. To understand why the European discovery led to such profound changes, we need to understand as best we can the nature of the native way of life and the knowledge the native peoples were able to bring to bear on the biggest event in their history: arrival of undreamed-of humans from out of the Pacific. This is a reverse view of the more common concern in our literature of the way in which the Europeans perceived and interpreted the New World they had found. Let us instead consider the way in which the aborigines saw and interpreted the coming of the Europeans,[1] with particular reference to the arrival of Sir Francis Drake, at this quadricentennial of his visit to California.

In this paper, I will review the historical evidence, examine the archaeological clues to the early explorations, and consider the Indian response to the arrival of the Europeans. The historical record is critical, for there is debate over just where the initial explorers were in California, and therefore uncertainty in some cases about which Indian groups they contacted. Particularly in the case of the Drake voyage, the debate goes on.

There are two bodies of evidence bearing on the location of contacts between Indians and Europeans along the California coast: the historical documents of the voyages, and material evidences in the archaeological record—sixteenth-century objects of Old World manufacture found in the ancient Indian villages. Unfortunately, all of this evidence is subject to alternative kinds of explanations, and unquestionable proof of exactly where many cultural contacts took place is still lacking. The body of evidence *is* sufficient for determination of the general tribal territory visited, even if we cannot yet put up a monument in the exact footprints of Cabrillo, Drake, or other early visitors to California.

Another relevant source of information is the recent ethnographic record with descriptive accounts of Indian customs and material possessions. The mention of such details in the historic accounts provides a way of identifying the Indian groups about which the explorers were talking.[2] Unfortunately, the early accounts are often no more thorough in describing Indians than they are at describing geographic details, so they rarely give us specific tribal identifications. Even so, from what is known of recent California Indians whose way of life has been studied in detail, it is feasible to identify not only the geographic locations of early visits, but also many details of the native way of life as it was in the sixteenth century. From this, in turn, may be derived a picture of the Indian viewpoint and response to arrival of the first Europeans on the shores of California.

The known sixteenth-century visits of Europeans are those of Cabrillo (1542), Drake (1579), and Cermeño (1595), with Vizcaíno (1602) just into the next century (I omit the Gulf of California explorations from this summary). There may have been other visitors to coastal California—unreported coastal visits by Manila galleons, or Spanish ships which disappeared after leaving Mexico on voyages to the north. It is also possible that some of the known voyagers might have put in to the California coast in unreported locations, perhaps in short visits to pick up food or water. In the absence of official and detailed logbooks, it is always possible that a brief anchorage of a couple of days could have been made without documentation in the historical accounts. Yet we certainly have records of the major visits, all of which have been exhaustively studied and documented by historians through many years of research. Only brief mention of the historical facts is given here to set the scene.[3]

Juan Rodríguez Cabrillo visited the California coast in 1542 and is generally considered the discoverer of California. He sailed the entire coastline of California, died on the voyage, and is buried on one of the channel islands off southern California.

Sir Francis Drake appeared off California in 1579, en route to the second circumnavigation of the globe and after a long voyage up the west coast of South America, raiding Spanish ships and settlements. He left from western Mexico, sailed northward along the coast to a point north of California, then returned and spent some weeks in a bay in central California in about 38° N latitude. After his stay in California, Drake sailed off across the Pacific and eventually back to England.

Sebastián Rodríguez Cermeño captained a galleon from Manila which put in to the California coast in 1595; it is generally agreed that he was at Drakes Bay north of San Francisco. Losing his ship in an onshore storm there, Cermeño took his crew to Acapulco in a small open sailboat.

The argument over the location of Drake's landfall in California has been going on for over a hundred years, beginning with an *Overland Monthly* article of 1868 claiming San Francisco Bay as the site of Drake's visit.[4] So much has been said and written about this controversy that it is not useful to review all the details here, particularly since the various arguments are well summarized in publications of the past few years.[5] Only a few additional comments can be added to this debate.

Although various points along the California coast have been suggested as the site of Drake's landing, today's scholars are unanimous, at least, in agreeing that the landing was somewhere in Marin County, just north of San Francisco. This now seems well established by two lines of evidence. First, there are the Drake accounts specifying the latitude of the landfall at near 38° N. There is no reason to doubt the correctness of this statement since latitude can be precisely determined from a simple sight on Polaris, Drake was a skilled navigator, and the normal errors of taking a star sight from a rolling ship did not apply since the Drake party was on shore for some weeks and had ample opportunity to check and recheck its position under the best of conditions (in spite of complaints about the summer fogs on the northern California coast, Drake's visit was long enough so that he must have had many opportunities for navigational sights). Even allowing for instrumental error and other uncertainties, Drake was certainly within twenty miles of where he said he was.

The second line of information, exploited by Kroeber, Heizer, and Elmendorf, among others,[6] involved a careful analysis of the description of the Indians seen by the Drake party—their language, clothing, and customs. From the bits of information recorded in the Drake accounts, there can be no doubt that Drake's party was in contact with Indians of central California, in all probability the tribe known as Coast Miwok, a finding which demonstrates the landing place to be in Marin County (or conceivably just barely north of the county line).

Unfortunately, this finding still includes sufficient coastline to allow for the possibility of four different bays as the site of

Drake's landing—from north to south they are Bodega Bay, Drakes Bay, Bolinas Bay, and San Francisco Bay. It is perhaps a historical detail of little consequence which one of these bays was the location of the Drake visit to California, but since the Drake voyage was a major event in California's history, and since there is a great desire to provide an adequate commemoration on the four hundredth anniversary in 1979, it would be very desirable to have some determination of precisely where Drake and his party set foot on the California coast, where they careened one of their boats, and where they lived and interacted with the Indians. The debate, which as mentioned above has gone on for a century, reached a crescendo in the last four or five years, with the supporters of one or the other of the possible landing sites putting forth their strongest arguments in print, public hearings, and formal written debate. Some of the scholars involved have changed their positions over the years, arguing for different locations as their interpretation of the various bits of evidence changed.

It is regrettable to conclude that we do not know the exact spot where Drake landed, and with all the exhaustive investigation to date, it seems even more regrettable to conclude that we *cannot* know for certain where the landing was made. Present evidence includes too many points of uncertainty and too many opportunities for legitimate differences in interpretation, and to find the exact landing place will require the discovery of new evidence, either in unknown historical documents, or possibly in archaeological findings of physical traces that can be unquestionably linked to the Drake party.

ARCHAEOLOGICAL EVIDENCES OF EARLY VOYAGERS TO
CALIFORNIA

It is axiomatic in archaeology that man will leave material traces of his occupancy of any place he visits. The finding of material relics of the earliest visitors to California not only would provide tangible evidences with great historical and museum value, but might also resolve some of the historical controversies about the exact places and peoples encountered in the age of exploration. Some considerable searching has been done to locate items that might have been left by the early voyagers; here these items and their claims to authenticity are reviewed.

For the earliest discoverer, Cabrillo, we might expect some objects of Spanish origin to have been left with the Indians, particularly in the offshore islands where several contacts were made and where Cabrillo is buried. There are two items that may derive from the Cabrillo expedition. By far the more important and interesting of these is the possible discovery of Cabrillo's tombstone—a large natural beach cobble with some crude and simple markings, originally collected on the surface in the early 1900s as part of a general survey of remains on Santa Rosa Island (fig. 1). This find remained largely unnoticed in the Lowie Museum at Berkeley for over sixty years, but has recently been analyzed and published by Heizer.[7] The marker is very simple, with crude and limited "inscription"; however, it is in keeping with what could be done in a sad little ceremony of burial on an island remote from any Spanish base in 1542. There are no known methods of scientific detective work that can ascertain the age of the stone or its markings, but it is too crude to be a deliberate falsification, and the best conclusion at present is that this *could be* the marker from the grave of California's discoverer. Regrettably, the finder did not record the exact location or leave records that would allow for further searching in the same place. Like all too many discoveries of this kind, it was not recognized to be of any particular significance and did not receive the attention it deserved.

Another possible evidence of Cabrillo's visit is a large glass trade bead—red, white, and blue, found on Catalina Island many years ago and now in the Southwest Museum, Los Angeles (fig. 2). There is no exact provenience, but it seems likely the bead was found at Avalon, where there was once a large Indian village. This is also the site of the harbor used by most human visitors. Glass beads were commonly carried as trinkets for gifts or trade with the natives, a custom initiated in the New World by Christopher Columbus. The bead in question is of the well-known "chevron" type, named from the colored chevrons seen on the faceted ends of the bead where the multicolored layers of glass are exposed. Such beads occur widely in six-

Fig. 1. Sandstone rock believed by Heizer to be a grave marker for Juan Rodríguez Cabrillo, found on Santa Rosa Island. Reproduced by permission, Lowie Museum of Anthropology, University of California, Berkeley.

Fig. 2. Glass trade bead from Catalina Island, length about one inch. These beads are made of varicolored layers of glass, in this case red, white, and blue—the tapered ends allow the lower layers to show through in a pattern of chevrons, giving the name "chevron bead" to this style of trade bead. There are many sizes and varieties in use for long periods as a trade item produced in Venice. This particular style is characteristic of sixteenth-century beads found widely in areas of Spanish exploration. From Catalina, this find is very likely attributable to the Cabrillo expedition of 1542. The specimen is in the Southwest Museum, Los Angeles, which permitted photography by the author.

teenth-century Spanish contexts ranging from Florida to Costa Rica, Peru, and Chile. It is unlikely that this particular type of chevron bead would have come to California after the middle of the sixteenth century, making the voyage of Cabrillo the logical source.

Tangible evidence of the Drake voyage includes a number of finds, and relics of this voyage have been diligently sought. Resolution of the controversies over Drake's landfall may ultimately rest on archaeological evidence since Drake was on the coast for some weeks and his account specifies that cloth and other things were given to the Indians, as well as mentions that he put up a brass plate claiming the land for Queen Elizabeth.

The debate over the Drake landing place has been complicated by the tangible clue that seemed at first to be the clincher: the Drake Plate, or "Plate of Brass," stated by the Drake accounts to have been erected on a "great and firme poste" to claim the land for the queen. The Drake Plate was reported to have been found near the shores of San Francisco Bay, but another claimant said he found it originally at Drakes Bay. Varying arguments over authenticity have also been made, with the latest opinion tipping in favor of considering the Drake Plate a hoax.[8] However, the report of James Hart of the Bancroft Library (where the plate now remains) concludes with the observation:

> Doubtless at later dates other inquiries and further commentary will be forthcoming from different sources to probe again into the nature and origin of an artifact that has attracted so much attention since its discovery.[9]

This is assuredly true, and the last word has not yet been said on the Drake Plate. However, in the problem of determining Drake's landing place, the issue of the Drake Plate has become almost irrelevant. For whether authentic or not the history of the finding is as full of controversy as other details of the Drake evidence, and final determinations about the Drake Plate are not likely to resolve the problem of where the "great and firme poste" was erected.

Related to the Drake Plate is the reported find of a sixteenth-century sixpence in a Marin County shellmound. The Drake account says that a sixpence was used as a seal for the territorial claim made by the plate of brass. Such a sixpence fits nicely into a jagged hole in the brass plate, and it is highly likely that the Indians would have collected both the plate and the sixpence and that sooner or later these items would find their way to an Indian village.

A much bigger find is the claimed Drake's Fort, a crudely walled small area at Bolinas Bay.[10] If this could be validated as a sixteenth-century construction, it would clinch the question of Drake's landing place. Unfortunately, there is not yet convincing evidence that the structure dates from so early a time.

Although extensive studies have been made of sixteenth-century Indian sites in several parts of Marin County,[11] small objects that might have been left by the Drake crew are remarkably few. The sixpence has been mentioned, but there are no glass beads or trinkets that can be identified with Drake. The cloth given to the Indians would not survive buried in an archaeological site, but there should be buttons or other small items that could be identified as English of the sixteenth century.[12] In addition, discarded materials like broken bottles are to be expected. Perhaps these will yet be found and they would be valuable historical relics. However, small and easily portable items cannot in themselves answer the question of where Drake landed, since such objects can easily turn up a great distance from where they were originally traded. The possibility that Drake could have left objects of Spanish or even Asian origin is discussed below with the finds attributed to the Cermeño visit.

In 1595, just sixteen years after the Drake voyage, Drakes Bay was visited by Sebastián Rodríguez Cermeño. Returning from a trip to the Philippines in one of the Manila galleons, Cermeño visited the California coast seeking a possible bay or way station that could be used to break the tremendously long and difficult Manila-to-Acapulco sea voyage. Unfortunately for him, but fortunately for the archaeological record, Cermeño lost his vessel, the *San Agustín,* in an onshore wind and returned to Mexico with his crew in a small open boat. The wrecked ship dispersed many material remains to be picked up by the Indians, resulting in many finds at several locations of Indian villages around Drakes Bay.

54

The most common objects preserved are pieces of blue-and-white Chinese porcelain of the Ming dynasty, representing broken vessels from the ship's cargo (fig. 3). The sherds were picked up on the beach by the Indians, who were no doubt attracted by the shiny blue-and-white pieces with their totally alien appearance to anything in the material culture of the Indians. Several hundred pieces have been found in seventeen separate sites. Most sherds were discarded in the village without use, but the Indians attempted to shape some pieces into beads, pendants, and other artifacts.[13]

Associated with the porcelain in the same sites have been found many badly rusted iron spikes, at least some of which are probably from the timbers of Cermeño's wrecked ship. None of these show any convincing evidence of use by the Indians, and they might well have come from pieces of ship's timbers carted into the villages and used as firewood. It is remarkable that the Indians apparently made no attempt to put the iron to use, since most stone-using peoples are quick to recognize the advantages of metal and utilize it in the manufacture of tools and weapons.

A metallurgical report on the spikes from the Drakes Bay sites concluded, "The iron spikes are undoubtedly of ancient origin."[14] It seems very probable that the iron objects do in fact date from the wreck of the *San Agustín* in 1595, but if they are indeed "ancient" it is equally possible that some could have come from the Drake expedition or even shipwrecks a century or two later. The chemical studies merely indicate that the wrought iron of the spikes is not recent: they do not provide a sixteenth-century date.

A humble but perhaps very significant find of sixteenth-century historic material from Drakes Bay is the occurrence of eleven pieces of the same large stoneware jar, all excavated from a small Indian village site on the Limantour Estero of Drakes Bay.[15] The sherds of this large brown-glazed jar are identified as of the sixteenth century and ultimately of Asian origin, and the presumption has been that the container was from a Manila ship, the most obvious identification being that it was from the *San Agustín,* source of the Chinese porcelain found in the same Indian village. However, the archaeological evidence is very clear that the pieces of the stoneware jar are buried significantly deeper in the archaeological deposit than the considerable num-

Fig. 3. Sherds of Ming dynasty Chinese porcelain from the 1595 shipwreck of the *San Agustín* in Drakes Bay (largest piece a little more than three inches across). These pieces are part of a collection of several hundred such finds from Indian sites around Drakes Bay; the illustrated specimens were photographed by the author in collections of the Lowie Museum, University of California, Berkeley.

ber of Ming porcelain fragments from this same location.[16] If the porcelain is linked to the 1595 wreck of Cermeño's ship, the stoneware must be older and must have reached Drakes Bay prior to 1595. Who could have carried it there? The only historically known visitors prior to Cermeño were Drake (1579) or possibly Cabrillo (1542). Although there is no record that Cabrillo landed here, he was this far north and might have made a stop for food or water. The only other possible source of the stoneware would be a ship of which no record exists, possibly even an Asian vessel.

That Drake could have been the bringer of the stoneware jar is evident in his taking of many jars from Spanish ships which were often stocked with such containers from the Manila trade. Kamer Aga-Oglu says that jars of the type excavated were used for "water or wine."[17] Drake took water containers from a Spanish ship off Central America on 10 April 1579,

> ... keeping onely one sailer [of all those captured] to shewe them where they should find fresh water, to the which ende they tooke the emptie vessels with them to fill with water. . . .[18]

Drake's ships then put in at Guatulco, leaving there on the sixteenth of April and proceeding to California where the landing was made 17 June.

The probabilities are therefore very high that Drake's ship arrived in California carrying water jars taken from the Spanish ships—maybe the pieces of such a jar from Drakes Bay are tangible evidence of Drake. (There is a small spring associated with the place the stoneware was found, making it a logical spot to fill water jars.)

Unfortunately, while it may be plausible to attribute the stoneware to the Drake visit, it cannot be proven that this was the source. This example is characteristic of the complexities and difficulties of interpreting archaeological finds. However, it also makes clear that we cannot confine our search to items "Made in England," for Drake was carrying all sorts of things from all over the world. Note that of the dozens of finds attributed to the Cermeño shipwreck, there is not a single item that has been demonstrated to be of Spanish or Mexican manufacture, and the same applies to the couple of finds that might

57

be linked to the Cabrillo voyage. Hence, the finding of "trade-mark" items that can be attributed only to a specific explorer is a most rare occurrence. (Incidentally, the Drake Plate is one such "trademark" item, which if genuine cannot be attributed to anything but the Drake expedition. From what has been said above, it may be relevant to note that chemical analysis of the Drake Plate cannot assume the plate to have originated in England—the brass items carried by Drake could have been fabricated by brass makers anywhere in the world.)

Just as no objects made for the Indian trade are known from the Drake expedition, so there are also no such items associated with the Cermeño voyage. There are no beads, hawksbells, knives, buttons, or any of the numerous items commonly used by the sixteenth-century Europeans to open up friendly relations with native peoples. Archaeologists hope that the lack of such trade items is a function of the incompleteness of the archaeological record, and of course such trade items may yet be found.

It is interesting, and may be significant, that Cermeño's account makes no mention of seeing any sign whatever of Drake's earlier visit to this coast only sixteen years before. Cermeño says nothing about seeing the Drake Plate on its post, Drake's Fort, or even any objects in possession of the Indians that might have been obtained from Europeans, such as metal tools. Politically, of course, the Spanish would not have recognized English intervention in what they considered to be their territory, but one might expect that a report to the Spanish authorities would certainly mention evidence of the English if any such evidence had in fact been seen. The differences between the Spanish and English accounts of Coast Miwok encounters have suggested to some that Drake and Cermeño were not in the same place, but this conclusion is by no means established beyond question.[19]

NATIVE RESPONSES TO THE ARRIVAL OF EUROPEANS

With some reasonable judgment of where the early explorers actually contacted the natives, one can attempt to reconstruct the world view and from this draw a picture of how the Indians must have reacted to the first alien visitors. Of course, such a reconstruction can be only a set of plausible interpretations—we cannot truly think with the minds of peoples so foreign to our own upbringing, peoples who left no written records and whose lifeways must be put together from the field observations of anthropologists (which themselves vary considerably in completeness and perceptiveness). Furthermore, we cannot know the influences of individual personalities of the time: the chiefs, shamans, and leaders to whom the people must have turned for guidance and explanation when strangers undreamt-of appeared suddenly from the sea.

The effort to see the era of exploration from the viewpoint of the Indians is nonetheless worthwhile. It not only provides a new perspective on the era of European expansion, but also allows us to interpret and explain some of the observations and comments made by the explorers themselves, who often could not understand native behavior they observed. Unfortunately, the early travelers were not ethnographers, did not spend much of their time in recording Indian ways, and in California were seldom in one place long enough to record the native customs, or even see them. Cermeño, in his return from Drakes Bay in 1595, sailed "close to the land and at times within a musket-shot of it," and seeing the whole coast of Marin County commented: "The land seemed to be unpopulated, as no people were seen on it in the day time, and at night there was no smoke nor fire."[20] This area of coast was certainly not uninhabited, but the small and scattered Indian villages were not seen by a coastal voyager.

Of the sixteenth-century accounts of contact with California Indians, the records of the Drake expedition are brief but surprisingly informative, and quite reliable in the light of modern knowledge. This discussion concentrates on the Drake contact with the Indians of northern California—a tribe demonstrated in previous discussion to have been the Coast Miwok. This small tribal group had never seen Europeans, nor indeed any peoples significantly different from themselves, yet their lives were forever altered with the appearance of England's pride, the redoubtable Sir Francis Drake, who lived among them for a few weeks in 1579.

Drake and his party knew the world was large and inhabited by very diverse peoples—they had seen many on their voyage to

California and were to see and deal with still more before completing their circumnavigation of the globe. To the Coast Miwok, the world was little—they used the resources of the coastline but did not venture out to sea, and most lived and died within a few miles of where they were born. The physical world of which they had direct knowledge included only their territory. The people of whom they had direct knowledge included only the neighboring tribes, peoples who spoke different languages but were basically like the Coast Miwok. A Coast Miwok drawing a map of the world could have included at most a few hundred square miles, a tiny world indeed compared to that being explored in the sixteenth century.

The native Californians of the time were remote and marginal peoples far from the centers of not only Old World, but also New World civilizations. As simple hunters and gatherers, their culture is marked by the absence of many features of human life considered basic to sixteenth-century Europeans—features which had already been present in European traditions for centuries or millenia. These included not only such skills as writing and the fabrication of metal objects, but even the knowledge of farming and the use of domestic animals. Even pottery was not known and cooking was done in baskets by dropping heated stones into the food. Native boats in this area were no more than small balsas made of reed bundles. The people's weapons were bows and arrows, their tools of chipped stone, their clothing rudimentary and often not much more than body paint, "although the paint is not so thick as with the Chichimecos."[21]

To the Indians, Drake and his men were not only strange people, but everything about them was at a marvelous degree of elaboration and technology—their great ship (small by European standards but far larger than any boat the Indians had ever imagined), their clothing and weapons, and even such simple domestic tools as metal knives, pottery jars, and woven cloth. The Indians were at first quite fearful of material objects possessed by the English, so much so that the first Indian who came off in a canoe to visit the anchored *Golden Hinde* took no presents of those offered by the English: ". . . he could not be drawne to receiue them by any meanes, saue one hat, which being cast into the water out of the ship, he tooke vp (refusing vtterly to meddle with any other thing, though it were vpon a board put off vnto him). . . ."[22] Later, an exchange took place, with the Indians given cloth and shirts and the English receiving baskets, arrows, and animal skins.

The social order of the Indians was also vastly simpler than that to which the English were accustomed. The Drake records refer several times to the "king" of the Indians: ". . . their king (making as princely a shew as possibly he could) with all his traine came forward."[23] It is also the basis for England's claim to the country that the "king" conceded the province into her majesty's hands. This was of course a false analogy to European concepts of nations and rulers. A common mistake extending down to the American period was the treating of Indian tribes as if they were "nations" with a central government, sharp political boundaries, and rulers comparable to those of the civilized world. This worked well enough in dealing with Indian civilizations such as those of the Aztecs or Incas, but it was entirely inappropriate for the simple hunting and gathering peoples like the Coast Miwok.

Ethnography of all the northern California Indians shows that these groups had no armies, police, or central political rulers. At most a Coast Miwok chief was a respected person whose advice was sought and whose influence extended over a maximum of a thousand persons or so, based entirely on personal leadership and without any force to compel others to do his will. Further, in this area where the people lived by hunting and gathering the resources provided by nature, the land was held in common and notions of private ownership of land were very weakly developed. To Europeans it made sense that a king could enter into treaties giving up territory, but this was not even conceivable in terms of the social system of the California Indians.

The population of the whole Coast Miwok group has been estimated by various scholars to be perhaps 2,000 to 4,000 at the time of the Spanish missions. Even assuming that number to be too low by a large margin, there could not have been more than a few thousand people of this group in 1579. The Drake accounts mention no community of any size, and although they mention a "great assembly" and "the greatest number of people which wee could reasonably imagine to dwell within any conuenient distance about," the only number given is with reference to the "king" and his "guard" of "about 100 tall and warlike men."[24] This probably included all of the initiated adult males from several villages, so the total number of Indians seen by the English is not likely to have been more than a few hundred.

The small population size and general simplicity of native communities are supported by the Drake accounts, describing the well-known houses of the precontact period extending down to historic times. The small native houses, "digged round within the earth," are described in detail with the further comment that there "being many of them in one place, [they] made seuerall villages here and there."[25]

From the Indian perspective, the English party was therefore impressively large in number and a considerable military force. Starting from England with 164 men, the Drake expedition was reduced by some losses so it is not known exactly how many men were in Drake's encampment in California. However, if the original party was reduced by as much as half, it was still about the size of the "king's guard" which as mentioned above probably included all the initiated men for some miles around. Military conflicts among the northern California Indians—primarily wars between villages—rarely had more than 100 persons on each side, so Drake's force would have appeared to the natives formidable in numbers alone. The Indians clearly did not see themselves as representing the "kingdom" defined by Drake; rather, they must have seen the force of strangers as more than sufficient to do what it wished in their territory.

It was in the realm of religious beliefs, however, that the English were unable to explain much of the Indian behavior they observed, just as the Indians were not fully able to understand what they saw of the English. Curiously, each side of this cross-cultural visit was able to see things they could interpret in terms of their own belief system—the appearances were similar although the meanings were different. For example, each group put forward its religious practitioners to make appropriate ceremonial observances for the other side. The Indians sent in their shaman to harangue the English with long speeches and appropriate gestures—the English offered prayers and sang psalms for the Indians, much to their delight. Since neither side could explain itself because of the language barrier, each could interpret the other's actions in its own frame of reference. Had someone in the English party been able to record in writing what the Indian shaman was saying, what a fascinating historical document would be available: a direct statement from the Indians of what they thought was happening. Unfortunately, no such statement exists, so the Indian viewpoint can be derived only from efforts to reconstruct it, such as this discussion.

The World Encompassed makes several mentions of the California natives' treatment of the English as supernatural beings: "wondring at vs as at gods" or some similar phrase occurs no less than seven times in the brief discussion of California. Such comments may be shrugged off as the mere ethnocentrism of the Europeans of the time, and the phraseology of the account sounds like something out of a mediocre movie dealing with civilized white men amongst the savages. Yet there is considerable evidence to indicate that the discussion in *The World Encompassed* is literally true and that the English correctly perceived the Indian reaction to them.

From the first contact, with a man in a canoe coming to the anchored *Golden Hinde,* the California Indians continually showed "reuerence and submission" to Drake's party, demonstrated by repeated offerings of ritually significant items. For example, the first Indian to approach the ship made an offering of a basket containing an herb, and along with this a bundle of black feathers tied into an ornament which Drake's records note was something "which they that guard their kings person weare on their heads." Heizer suggests that this was a feather bundle associated with the central religion of Californians: the Kuksu cult.[26] The description is consistent with such an interpretation, and I believe the feather bundle was a "magpie" of the kind worn by contemporary Pomo dancers in religious ceremonies.[27] The herb in the basket is not identifiable today, but can be presumed to be a ritual item rather than something used in ordinary commerce. Tobacco would be a logical offering, and since the English recorded the name of the herb as "tobah" or "tabah," it has been interpreted by some that the herb was in fact tobacco. This interpretation is challenged on linguistic grounds, the local languages having different words for "tobacco." Hence, the herb

63

offered by the Indian might have been tobacco, but it is just as likely that it was angelica root or any one of a number of other plants having ritual value for the Indians.

It is clear that the Indian delivering these offerings refused to accept presents in return, so this contact was not for purposes of trade, nor would it be mere hospitality to visitors since in the latter case food would be the normal gift.

Other examples of "offerings" occur in the Drake accounts. More significant is the behavior of the Indians when Drake landed and came in contact with groups of Indian visitors. An early reaction was a "bloudie sacrifice" described so graphically in *The World Encompassed:*

> ... the women ... vsed vnnatural violence against themselues, crying and shrieking piteously, tearing their flesh with their nailes from their cheekes in a monstrous manner, the blood streaming downe along their brests ... they would with furie cast themselues vpon the ground, neuer respecting whether it were cleane or soft, but dashed themselues in this manner on hard stones, knobby hillocks, stocks of wood, and pricking bushes ... itterating the same course againe and againe; yea women great with child, some nine or ten times each, and others holding out till 15 or 16 times (till their strengths failed them) exercised this cruelty against themselues....

On a later occasion, the people

> ... dispersed themselues among our people, taking a diligent view or suruey of euery man; and finding such as pleased their fancies (which commonly were the youngest of vs), they presently enclosing them about offred their sacrifices vnto them, crying out with lamentable shreekes and moanes, weeping and scratching and tearing their very flesh off their faces with their nailes.... [28]

These descriptions pertain to the usual behavior of Indians at the death of someone, lamentations and mortification of the flesh (particularly by the women) being the usual mourning behavior. Both Kroeber and Heizer have interpreted this Indian reaction to Drake and his men as explainable on the supposition by the Indians that they were looking at people returned from the land of the dead, an interpretation entirely consistent with native religion and mythology in central California. The Drake accounts clearly recognize that the English were being treated as "gods," but they do not show any English awareness that the reason for this behavior was an Indian interpretation that the English were ghosts or spirits, and that their careful scrutiny of individuals was a search for departed relatives returned from the dead. Of course, any fancied resemblances between departed Indians and Drake's men would be with the "youngest of vs," for few Indians lived to an advanced age (the average age of death in this hunter-gatherer culture certainly being less than thirty-five).

Some specific details of the belief system of the Coast Miwok support the plausibility of this interpretation. Coast Miwok tales collected by Kelly state that the land of Coyote (the creator) was far to the west, beyond the ocean, and further that Coyote went across the ocean "where the sun sets," and there the dead go to be with him. The stories specifically place the beginning of the path to the afterworld at Point Reyes: "The dead go toward Point Reyes and go down there. . . . A piece of rock about two feet long is at the spot where they jump into the ocean and then follow a road back of the breakers."[29]

Given such beliefs and the limited knowledge of the external world held by the peoples of California in the sixteenth century, what other conclusion could be drawn by the Indians but that people were returning from the land of the dead? A ship larger and more elaborate than anything known to the Indians, carrying men of pale complexion with strange clothing and material goods, arriving out of the western sea where the spirits began their journey to the afterworld, could only be seen as the arrival of a boatload of ghosts. What a shock! It is too bad we will never know what the Indian leaders and shamans of the time said to the people about this shattering experience, and a terrible loss to history that the English were unable to record the speeches and harangues of the Indians expressing their efforts to cope with this astonishing experience. What the Indians *did*, however, is clearly recorded, and their actions were those associated with death and mourning—offerings, solemn orations, and mortification of the flesh.

From all this evidence, we can infer that the Indians of sixteenth-century California saw the arrival of Europeans as the

65

kind of event that portends the end of the world. In terms of *their* world, they were right.[30]

Notes

1. There are many publications dealing with the way in which the discovery of the New World changed man's life in the Old World, and with the perceptions of America as seen by the European explorers. See, for example, Fredi Chiappelli, ed., *First Images of America: The Impact of the New World on the Old*, 2 vols. (Berkeley: University of California Press, 1976); Hugh Honour, *The New Golden Land: European Images of America from the Discoveries to the Present Time* (New York: Pantheon Books, 1975). No really comparable volumes consider the matter from the other side and treat of the first images of Europeans by the Indians. This is, of course, largely because of the absence of a literary tradition in the aboriginal New World—the Indians were not writing books about the Europeans nor publishing pictures of them. There are some interesting but widely scattered examples of native art portraying Europeans, but any effort to visualize the way in which the early Indians saw the arrival of the Europeans must perforce be based on knowledge of Indian ethnography—a second-hand reconstruction rather than a contemporary document from the age of exploration. Any effort to reconstruct Indian attitudes of hundreds of years ago must therefore be quite limited. These limitations also apply to interpretations of the Indian mentality and world view written by contemporary Indian authors, since their often polemical treatment of the subject deals primarily with the effects of long-term contact between Indians and Europeans, not with the initial impact or the efforts of the native people to understand and formulate what was happening when alien peoples first came into their world.

2. Convincing use of the ethnographic record has been applied by several anthropologists with respect to the Drake voyage. For California, see Robert F. Heizer, *Francis Drake and the California Indians, 1579*, University of California Publications in American Archaeology and Ethnology, vol. 42, no. 3, pp. 251–302 (Berkeley, 1947). The ethnographic record has also been used to identify other areas visited by Drake, since his journey was largely made without benefit of maps, charts, or previous geographic knowledge and he was the first European to visit many of the native peoples he encountered. His Pacific landing places have been well studied by William A. Lessa, *Drake's Island of Thieves: Ethnological Sleuthing* (Honolulu: University Press of Hawaii, 1975).

3. The primary sources for these voyages are not cited in detail here; they are all readily available through standard summaries such as Samuel Eliot Morison, *The European Discovery of America*, 2 vols. (New York: Oxford University Press, 1971–74). See also John W. Robertson, *Francis Drake and Other Early Explorers along the Pacific Coast* (San Francisco: Grabhorn Press, 1927) and Henry R. Wagner, *Sir Francis Drake's Voyage around the World: Its Aims and Achievements* (San Francisco: John Howell, 1926).

4. J. D. B. Stillman, "Did Drake Discover San Francisco Bay?" *Overland Monthly* 1 (1868): 332–37.

5. The most recent review of the evidence is Warren L. Hanna, *Lost Harbor: The Controversy over Drake's California Anchorage* (Berkeley: University of California Press, 1979). All sides are represented in the debate edited by Marilyn Ziebarth, *The Francis Drake Controversy: His California Anchorage, June 17–July 23, 1579*, in *California Historical Quarterly* 53, no. 3 (1974): 197–292. It is unnecessary to cite here the individual articles by proponents for one or another of the possible landing sites, since they are documented and their viewpoints well expressed in the summary treatments referenced above.

6. In addition to the references in note 2, see Alfred L. Kroeber, *Handbook of the Indians of California*, Smithsonian Institution, Bureau of American Ethnology Bulletin no. 78 (Washington, 1925; reprint eds., Berkeley: California Book Company, 1953, 1970; paperback ed., New York: Dover Books, 1976); Robert F. Heizer and William W. Elmendorf, "Francis Drake's California Anchorage in the Light of the Indian Language Spoken There," *Pacific Historical Review* 11, no. 2 (1942): 213–17.

7. Robert F. Heizer, *California's Oldest Historical Relic?* (Berkeley: Robert H. Lowie Museum of Anthropology, University of California, 1972).

8. The literature on the Drake Plate is extensive. Aside from general opinions and evaluations, see *The Plate of Brass: Evidence of the Visit of Francis Drake to California in the Year 1579*, California Historical Society Special Publication no. 25 (San Francisco, 1953); Colin G. Fink and E. P. Polushkin, *Drake's Plate of Brass Authenticated: The Report on the Plate of Brass*, California Historical Society Special Publication no. 14 (San Francisco, 1938; reprinted in the 1953 special publication just cited); Allen L. Chickering, "Further Notes on the Drake Plate," *California Historical Society Quarterly* 18, no. 3 (1939): 251–52; Helen V. Michel and Frank Asaro, *Chemical Study of the Plate of Brass*, Lawrence Laboratory Publication LBL-6338 (Berkeley, 1977); James D. Hart, *The Plate of Brass Reexamined* (Berkeley: Bancroft Library, 1977); Robert H. Power, "A Plate of Brass by Me . . . C. G. Francis Drake," *California History* 57, no. 2 (1978): 172–85.

9. Hart, *Plate of Brass Reexamined*, p. 25.

10. V. Aubrey Neasham and William E. Pritchard, *Drake's California Landing: The Evidence for Bolinas Lagoon* (Sacramento: Western Heritage, 1974).

11. Edward P. von der Porten and Rene K. Peron, *Archaeology in the Point Reyes National Seashore* (Point Reyes, Calif.: Drake Navigators Guild, 1973); Clement W. Meighan and Robert F. Heizer, "Archaeological Exploration of Sixteenth-Century Indian Mounds at Drake's Bay," *California Historical Society Quarterly* 31, no. 2 (1952): 98–108, reprinted in California Historical Society Special Publication no. 25, *The Plate of Brass*, pp. 73–81. These discussions review sites associated with artifacts of the Cermeño voyage. Many sites of the historic and protohistoric period are known and partially published, including Olompali (central Marin County), the Thomas Site (near San Quentin), and additional Drakes Bay locations studied by A. E. Treganza of San Francisco State University. The interest in the historical relics, however, has dominated research in this area and most of the reporting of the aboriginal archaeology is yet to be done.

12. Edward von der Porten, *Drake and Cermeño in California: Sixteenth-Century Chinese Ceramics* (Point Reyes, Calif.: Drake Navigators Guild, 1973; this article also appears in *Historical Archaeology* 6 [1972]: 1–22). Mention is made (p. 7) of a small group of finds that are suggested as possibly derived from the Drake camp, including a copper cone, an iron bar, and a fragment of wool cloth. The same site includes porcelain and iron spikes from the Cermeño shipwreck. This points up the extreme difficulty of segregating historic finds and attributing them to specific visits in an area where several possible visitors could have left behind nondescript items of everyday use.

13. The most detailed studies of the oriental porcelain fragments are the article cited in note 12 above and Edward von der Porten, *The Porcelains and Terra Cottas of Drakes Bay* (Point Reyes, Calif.: Drake Navigators Guild, 1968). In the latter report, Appendix 1 tabulates 651 sherds of sixteenth-century porcelains from seventeen locations. A few sherds were found on beaches and at scattered locations, but the great majority are from fifteen archaeological sites representing Indian villages formerly located around Drakes Bay; the number of porcelain finds per site ranges from 1 to 238 pieces. The origin of these fragments from a shipwreck is clearly demonstrated by the beach finds, the water-worn condition of many sherds, and the absence of complete or reasonably complete porcelain vessels (although some scattered sherds fit together, permitting partial reconstruction of two or three bowls). It is clear that the pieces were not traded to the Indians, but were picked up from the beaches and taken to the villages as curiosities.

A few additional pieces have been found since the 1968 study; see Edward von der Porten, *Two Oriental Porcelain Sherds from Olompali, Marin County, California* (Point Reyes, Calif.: Drake Navigators Guild, 1976).

This is significant as a rare find of porcelain at an inland site away from the shores of Drakes Bay; it indicates contact between the Drakes Bay villages and the site of Olompali some miles inland.

Von der Porten, *Drake and Cermeño in California,* states that the historical artifacts of Drakes Bay "were scattered at all depths in the middens, so no physical sixteenth-century level could be located." To the extent this is true, it results partly from site disturbance and partly from insufficient care in recording the exact depth at which the historic artifacts were found. However, there is considerable evidence to recognize sixteenth-century levels in Drakes Bay sites. Von der Porten recognized such a level in his own 1968 work, and my own excavations show that there are recognizable stratigraphic units associated with the sixteenth-century visits. My limited work at Mrn-232 clearly shows that the sixteenth-century artifacts are heavily concentrated in the top twelve inches of the midden. At nearby site Mrn-307, which is almost wholly excavated, the average depth of twenty-seven fragments of porcelain was only seven inches and eleven of the pieces were less than five inches in depth—essentially on the surface in the roots of the grass and weeds which cover the site.

Since dwellers on a shell midden can accumulate a foot of deposit in only a few years, it cannot be expected that a very thin sixteenth-century level will be recognizable or that we will be able to pinpoint such a level to within a centimeter. However, the stratigraphic picture is not really obscure and it reveals significant conclusions. The site of Mrn-307, for example, was clearly abandoned within a very short time (certainly no more than a few years) after the 1595 visit of the Spanish. This appears to be also true for some other sites in this area, some of which were never again inhabited, and some of which were reoccupied after a period of abandonment. It may well be that there was a marked population decline at the end of the sixteenth century, directly brought about by introduced European diseases, which had devastating effects in many Indian populations. This is not historically documented at Drakes Bay since the early explorers did not stay there long enough to observe such an effect, but it is well documented in many other regions of the New World.

14. Robert F. Heizer, "Archaeological Evidence of Sebastián Rodríguez Cermeño's California Visit in 1595," *California Historical Society Quarterly* 20, no. 4 (1941): 315–28, reprinted as a separate pamphlet by the California Historical Society, 1942. Appended to this study is the analysis of the wrought-iron spikes: Colin G. Fink and Eugene P. Polushkin, "Report on the Examination of Ten Iron Spikes Recently Found at Drake's Bay, California." The specimens analyzed were from the Estero Site (Mrn-232); many more examples of iron spikes were recovered from the mound than those studied, and they have also been found in several other Drakes Bay sites. Some years after publication of the report just cited, Professor Fink examined some large iron rods found buried in another Indian site (Mrn-307) within a couple of hundred yards of the find-spot of the

previously analyzed specimens. He concluded that the large iron rods were recent (the same site also contains examples of the small wrought-iron spikes characteristic of the nearby Estero Site). It is possible that modern trace-element studies could provide a more definitive answer on the age and origin of the iron objects from Drakes Bay sites. The conclusion that most of these objects come from the wreck of Cermeño's ship is based in large part on their archaeological associations with the Ming porcelain fragments, since few of the iron objects have been intensively studied and the results of the analyses are somewhat equivocal. So far, the evidence of the iron objects themselves does not provide a firm sixteenth-century dating, unlike the Chinese porcelain, which is well dated.

15. See references cited in note 11 above. The Meighan and Heizer article includes an appendix: Kamer Aga-Oglu, "Fragments of a Stoneware Jar Found at Drake's Bay, California" (pp. 106–8; reprint, pp. 79–81).

16. Von der Porten, *Porcelains and Terra Cottas,* takes issue with the stratigraphic data reported for Mrn-307 and dismisses the differences in depth of the porcelain and stoneware fragments as meaningless. He suggests that the greater depth of the stoneware fragments is due to their larger size and that they somehow sank down into the ground more than the lighter porcelain pieces. It is a very naive, but widely held, idea that heavy objects sink to the bottom of an archaeological site. This has never been demonstrated in any archaeological site and if it were true it would make all archaeological stratigraphy valueless. Objects get moved around in archaeological sites from three main causes: aboriginal digging (for graves, etc.), plant roots, and (most important in California), the actions of burrowing animals such as gophers and ground squirrels. If it were not for the diligence of the latter over centuries of tunneling, we would have a near-perfect stratigraphy at many Drakes Bay sites. However, contrary to von der Porten's suggestion, the larger and heavier an item is, the less likely it is to be moved from the place where it was deposited.

The evidence is quite strong that the stoneware fragments at Mrn-307 got to Drakes Bay at some time prior to the 1595 porcelain in the same site. Establishing this point, however, does not identify when the stoneware arrived or who brought it, and conclusions on these points are necessarily speculative. On the other hand, it flies in the face of the evidence to argue that the stoneware came to Drakes Bay in 1595 with Cermeño. This is possible only if someone at that time was digging holes and burying the stoneware—an unlikely possibility and one for which there is no evidence.

17. "Fragments of a Stoneware Jar," p. 107; reprint, p. 80 (see note 15).

18. N. M. Penzer, ed., *The World Encompassed and Analogous Contemporary Documents concerning Sir Francis Drake's Circumnavigation of*

the World (New York: Cooper Square Publishers, 1969), p. 180. The California parts of the Drake account have been reprinted many times and occur in several of the California Historical Society publications, including the "debate" edited by Marilyn Ziebarth, cited in note 5.

19. The Ziebarth item cited in note 5 also includes a reprinting of the Cermeño observations in California as translated by Wagner.

The difference between the reported observations and experiences of the Drake and Cermeño visits (in such things as the number of people seen, the animals observed, and the behavior of the Indians toward the Europeans) has caused some to question whether these visits could have been to the same location. Robert H. Power, "Cermeño and Drake, Did They Anchor in the Same Harbor" (Manuscript submitted to the California Historical Resources Commission, 1976), argues that Drake's anchorage must have been elsewhere than near Point Reyes. This is a matter worth serious examination, but the documentation of the early accounts is insufficient for a resolution of the question. It must also be remembered that the Drake visit was in June–July and the Cermeño party was on the coast in November–December. Not only plants and animals, but also Indian populations fluctuated markedly between summer and winter as the Indians moved in a seasonal round of hunting and plant collecting. Hence, the observations of summer and winter visitors might well be very different. For example, much has been made of Drake's observation of a multitude of "conies"— surely a reference to the California ground squirrel. These are seen in quantity only in the summer, and their numbers vary a great deal from year to year. The fact that Cermeño made no mention of "conies" therefore does not establish that he was in a different bay, nor even that Drake had to be in the region where ground squirrels are today most abundant. Like so many aspects of early explorers' accounts, the differences between the Drake and Cermeño accounts remain puzzling and not fully explainable.

20. In Ziebarth, *Francis Drake Controversy,* p. 288.

21. Ibid.

22. See Penzer, *World Encompassed,* p. 53. It is interesting that the only item the Indian took was a hat that had fallen into the water. It is a standard Indian belief in California, documented in several areas including that of the Pomo bordering on Coast Miwok territory, that objects containing "power," and hence dangerous, can be disarmed and made safe by immersing them in water. Regalia of a dead shaman, for example, are disposed of under water by being sunk in a lake. Perhaps the Indian visiting Drake's ship was not afraid to touch the hat and take it with him because it was floating in the water and had therefore lost any dangerous spiritual power it might have contained. A somewhat analogous Christian belief is the overcoming of evil forces by the use of holy water, as in the Dracula story.

It is noteworthy that the Indians later returned to Drake's party all gifts they had received after the English landed, "none carrying with him anything of whatsoeuer hee had receiued" (ibid., p. 56; Heizer, *Francis Drake and the California Indians*, p. 273). Heizer also notes the recording of an Indian phrase, "nocharo mu" = "touch me not" (see pp. 273–74). All of this clearly indicates the Indians to have been very fearful of the English and to have viewed contact with them or their material goods as dangerous. This is part of a common concept of "danger" associated with shamans, dancers, and ritual regalia in central California Indian beliefs. Even to see such items could lead to sickness or death for an uninitiated or improperly prepared person.

In view of the great difficulties we have had in finding archaeological evidences of the Drake visit, we might wish the Miwok had been more avaricious and acquisitive of European goods; their behavior indicates one reason why material relics of Drake will be few and far between.

23. Penzer, *World Encompassed*, p. 57.

24. Ibid., pp. 56, 57.

25. Ibid., pp. 54, 62.

26. Ibid., p. 53; Heizer, *Francis Drake and the California Indians*, p. 261.

27. The knowledge of what the Indian belief system was like in the sixteenth century depends upon recent survivals of many of the cultural features observed by the Drake party. Since the area north of San Francisco felt few effects of Spanish missionizing until about 1800, and was never really colonized by the Spanish, it was possible for tribes of the area to preserve much of their religion and mythology down to this century. While aboriginal Coast Miwok culture died out early and can be considered extinct, informants for this group were still available until the 1930s and anthropological data could be collected from them by such anthropologists as A. L. Kroeber and Isabel Kelly. The Pomo, a closely similar tribal group whose territory borders on Coast Miwok, maintain their language and much of their belief system to the present day. The Pomo have been studied by many anthropologists, and details of the religious system appear in several monographs. For a recent example, see Clement W. Meighan and Francis A. Riddell, *The Maru Cult of the Pomo Indians, a California Ghost Dance Survival*, Southwest Museum Papers no. 23 (Los Angeles, 1972). This volume reports some specific ceremonial practices observed by Drake, among them the cry of approbation, "Oh!" given by the congregation to songs and orations. This custom, still present in Indian gatherings today, was observed by Drake—the Indian populace cried "Oh!" for the psalms sung by the English, seeing such music as comparable to their own ritually oriented singing.

28. Penzer, *World Encompassed,* pp. 56, 60.

29. Isabel Kelly, "Some Coast Miwok Tales," *Journal of California Anthropology* 5, no. 1 (1978): 21–41; the quotations are from pp. 24, 39.

30. Although it was to be some two centuries after the Drake visit before there was any significant intrusion or settlement of Coast Miwok territory, it is likely that severe disruption of the Indian culture was the result of the sixteenth-century visits. The psychological impact is well documented, and we have to consider the possibility of disease-introduction as well (see the discussion in note 13 of the abandonment of some Drakes Bay sites shortly after the initial contact with European explorers).

Members of the Seminar

Page Ackerman
Raymond Aker
Michael Allen
Mr. & Mrs. Ogden B. Armour
Daniel Arreola
Mr. & Mrs. Harold W. Axe
Mr. & Mrs. John F. Barrows
Mr. & Mrs. David S. Berkowitz
Mr. & Mrs. Ray A. Billington
Robert H. Block
Henry J. Bruman
Edwin H. Carpenter
Tony Cimolino
Mr. & Mrs. William E. Conway
Vera Cornell
Charlotte Crabtree
David Cressy
James G. Davis
Mr. & Mrs. Glen Dawson
Noel L. Diaz
Mr. & Mrs. Benjamin Draper
Shoshanah Dubiner
Mr. & Mrs. Gary S. Dunbar
Richard Enthoven
Raymond H. Fisher
Rosemary Ford
Winifred Freese
Frances W. Fry
J. Thomas Frye
Henry Goodman
Mr. & Mrs. Everett G. Hager
Neal Harlow
Dr. & Mrs. Charles Heiskell

David A. Henderson
Mr. & Mrs. W. O. Hendricks
Mr. & Mrs. E. W. Holland
Mr. & Mrs. Alfred Horn
Mr. & Mrs. Norris Hundley
J. Roger Jobson
John H. Kemble
Dorothy Kuhn
Mr. & Mrs. Ludwig Lauerhass
Karen Lence
Harry A. Levinson
Mr. & Mrs. James Lightfoot
Mr. & Mrs. George Lindsay
Richard F. Logan
Gloria R. Lothrop
Patrick J. McCloskey
David McJunkin
Mr. & Mrs. Tom L. McKnight
Lois Matthews
Clement W. Meighan
Andy Mitchell
Mr. & Mrs. Everett T. Moore
Kenneth Muir
Mr. & Mrs. Howard J. Nelson
Blake Nevius
Mr. & Mrs. Robert Newcomb
Mr. & Mrs. Alfred W. Newman
Ada B. Nisbet
Beverly Onley
Mr. & Mrs. James Phillips
Owen Pinckney
Mr. & Mrs. John O. Pohlmann
Mr. & Mrs. Robert H. Power

75

Saleem Rana
John D. Rees
Frances Ring
Donald Roberts
Mary Robertson
Ernest P. Rook
Mr. & Mrs. Alan Roper
Mr. & Mrs. Jonathan Sauer
Jean Ford Schilling
Mr. & Mrs. Donald L. Segal
Nancy Malim Shea
Matthew Silberman
Mr. & Mrs. Eli Sobel
Mr. & Mrs. Joseph E. Spencer
Elizabeth Swedenberg
Mr. & Mrs. John Swingle
Neady C. Taylor
Mr. & Mrs. Donald R. Thieler
Benjamin E. Thomas

Mr. & Mrs. Norman J. W. Thrower
Mr. & Mrs. Gerald E. Tyner
Esmeralda Vallejo
Ralph Vicero
Mr. & Mrs. Robert Vosper
Helen Wallis
David W. Waters
John D. Weaver
Mr. & Mrs. Jeff Weber
Mr. & Mrs. Roby Wentz
Lyndon Wester
Mr. & Mrs. Lynn T. White, Jr.
F. Brooke Whiting
Raymund F. Wood
Thomas F. Wright
Ramin Bet Younan
Suellen Zecchini
Mr. & Mrs. Jacob Zeitlin
Mr. & Mrs. Marion A. Zeitlin

William Andrews Clark Memorial Library Seminar Papers

Editing Donne and Pope. 1952.
  Problems in the Editing of Donne's Sermons, by George R. Potter.
  Editorial Problems in Eighteenth-Century Poetry, by John Butt.
Music and Literature in England in the Seventeenth and Eighteenth Centuries. 1953.
  *Poetry and Music in the Seventeenth Century, by James E. Phillips.
  *Some Aspects of Music and Literature in the Eighteenth Century, by Bertrand H. Bronson.
Restoration and Augustan Prose. 1956.
  *Restoration Prose, by James R. Sutherland.
  *The Ironic Tradition in Augustan Prose from Swift to Johnson, by Ian Watt.
Anglo-American Cultural Relations in the Seventeenth and Eighteenth Centuries. 1958.
  *The Puritans in Old and New England, by Leon Howard.
  William Byrd: Citizen of the Enlightenment, by Louis B. Wright.
The Beginnings of Autobiography in England, by James M. Osborn. 1959.
Scientific Literature in Sixteenth and Seventeenth Century England. 1961.
  English Medical Literature in the Sixteenth Century, by C. D. O'Malley.
  English Scientific Literature in the Seventeenth Century, by A. Rupert Hall.
Francis Bacon's Intellectual Milieu. A Paper delivered by Virgil K. Whitaker at a meeting at the Clark Library, 18 November 1961, celebrating the 400th anniversary of Bacon's birth.
Methods of Textual Editing, by Vinton A. Dearing. 1962.
The Dolphin in History. 1963.
  The History of the Dolphin, by Ashley Montagu.

Modern Whales, Dolphins, and Porpoises, as Challenges to Our Intelligence, by John G. Lilly.

Thomas Willis as a Physician, by Kenneth Dewhurst. 1964.

History of Botany. 1965.
Herbals, Their History and Significance, by George H. M. Lawrence.
A Plant Pathogen Views History, by Kenneth F. Baker.

Neo-Latin Poetry of the Sixteenth and Seventeenth Centuries. 1965.
Daniel Rogers: A Neo-Latin Link between the Pléiade and Sidney's 'Areopagus,' by James E. Phillips.
*Milton as a Latin Poet, by Don Cameron Allen.

Milton and Clarendon: Papers on Seventeenth-Century English Historiography. 1965.
Milton as Historian, by French R. Fogle.
Clarendon and the Practice of History, by H. R. Trevor-Roper.

Some Aspects of Seventeenth Century English Printing with Special Reference to Joseph Moxon, by Carey S. Bliss. 1965.

Homage to Yeats, 1865–1965. 1966.
Yeats and the Abbey Theatre, by Walter Starkie.
Women in Yeats's Poetry, by A. Norman Jeffares.

Alchemy and Chemistry in the Seventeenth Century. 1966.
Renaissance Chemistry and the Work of Robert Fludd, by Allen G. Debus.
Some Nonexistent Chemists of the Seventeenth Century, by Robert P. Multhauf.

The Uses of Irony. 1966.
*Daniel Defoe, by Maximillian E. Novak.
*Jonathan Swift, by Herbert J. Davis.

Bibliography. 1966.
Bibliography and Restoration Drama, by Fredson Bowers.
In Pursuit of American Fiction, by Lyle H. Wright.

Words to Music. 1967.
English Song and the Challenge of Italian Monody, by Vincent Duckles.
Sound and Sense in Purcell's 'Single Songs,' by Franklin B. Zimmerman.

John Dryden. 1967.
*Challenges to Dryden's Biographer, by Charles E. Ward.
*Challenges to Dryden's Editor, by H. T. Swedenberg.

Atoms, Blacksmiths, and Crystals. 1967.
> The Texture of Matter as Viewed by Artisan, Philosopher, and Scientist in the Seventeenth and Eighteenth Centuries, by Cyril Stanley Smith.
>
> Snowflakes and the Constitution of Crystalline Matter, by John G. Burke.

Laplace as a Newtonian Scientist, by Roger Hahn. 1967.

Modern Fine Printing. 1968.
> The Private Press: Its Essence and Recrudescence, by H. Richard Archer.
>
> Tradition and Southern California Printers, by Ward Ritchie.

Medical Investigation in Seventeenth Century England. 1968.
> Embryological Thought in Seventeenth Century England, by Charles W. Bodemer.
>
> Robert Boyle as an Amateur Physician, by Lester S. King.

The Life and Works of Eric Gill. 1968.
> Reminiscences, by Cecil Gill.
>
> Eric Gill, Typographer, by Beatrice Warde.
>
> Mr. Gill, by David Kindersley.

The Flow of Books and Manuscripts. 1969.
> The Case of the "Caxton" Manuscript of Ovid: Reflections on the Legislation Controlling the Export of Works of Art from Great Britain, by A. N. L. Munby.
>
> Every Silver Lining Has a Cloud: The Shaping of the Newberry's Collection, by Lawrence W. Towner.

Some Aspects of Seventeenth-Century Medicine and Science. 1969.
> Van Helmont, Boyle, and the Alkahest, by Ladislao Reti.
>
> The Medical Interests of Christopher Wren, by William C. Gibson.

The Terraqueous Globe: The History of Geography and Cartography. 1969.
> Edmond Halley and Thematic Geo-Cartography, by Norman J. W. Thrower.
>
> On Chateaubriand's Journey in 1806 from Paris to Jerusalem, by Clarence J. Glacken.

The Task of the Editor. 1969.
> The Ideal of Textual Criticism, by James Thorpe.
>
> The Practice of Textual Criticism, by Claude M. Simpson, Jr.

The Lady of Letters in the Eighteenth Century. 1969.
> *Letters of Advice to Young Spinsters, by Irvin Ehrenpreis.
>
> *Ladies of Letters in the Eighteenth Century, by Robert Halsband.

The Private Collector and the Support of Scholarship. 1969.
The Book Collector as Public Benefactor, by Louis B. Wright.
The Private Collector and the Literary Scholar, by Gordon N. Ray.
Hobbes and the Epic Tradition of Political Theory, by Sheldon S. Wolin. 1970.
Influences on California Printing. 1970.
The Book Club of California: Its Impress on Fine Printing, by James D. Hart.
The Primavera Press, by Ward Ritchie.
The Primavera Press: A Bibliography, by J. M. Edelstein.
Charles Dickens and George Cruikshank. 1971.
The Fiction of Realism: *Sketches by Boz, Oliver Twist,* and Cruikshank's Illustrations, by J. Hillis Miller.
George Cruikshank: Mirror of an Age, by David Borowitz.
Some Aspects of Eighteenth-Century England. 1971.
Reason and Unreason in the Eighteenth Century: The English Experience, by J. H. Plumb.
A Walk through London with John Gay and a Run with Daniel Defoe, by Vinton A. Dearing.
Congreve Consider'd. 1971.
The "just Decrees of Heav'n" and Congreve's *Mourning Bride,* by Aubrey Williams.
Love, Scandal, and the Moral Milieu of Congreve's Comedies, by Maximillian E. Novak.
Theology in Sixteenth- and Seventeenth-Century England. 1971.
Fast Days and Civil Religion, by Winthrop S. Hudson.
A.D. 1689: The End of the Clerical World, by Leonard J. Trinterud.
English and Continental Views of the Ottoman Empire 1500–1800. 1971.
The Double Veil: Travelers' Views of the Ottoman Empire, Sixteenth through Eighteenth Centuries, by Ezel Kural Shaw.
Sir Paul Rycaut, A Seventeenth-Century Observer of the Ottoman State: Notes for a Study, by C. J. Heywood.
Checklist of Turcica in the Clark Library, compiled by William E. Conway.
Changing Taste in Eighteenth-Century Art and Literature. 1972.
The Art of Piranesi: Looking Backward into the Future, by Robert E. Moore.
"Such, Such Were the Joys": The Boyhood of the Man of Feeling, by Jean H. Hagstrum.
French and English Drama of the Seventeenth Century. 1972.
Tears of Magnanimity in Otway and Racine, by Eugene M. Waith.

80

From Corneille to Molière: The Metaphor of Value, by Judd D. Hubert.

English Satire. 1972.

Martin Marprelate: His Identity and Satire, by Leland H. Carlson.

Satire, and Poetry, and Pope, by Ronald Paulson.

The Editor as Critic and the Critic as Editor. 1973.

Critical Problems in Editing George Herbert's *The Temple*, by J. Max Patrick.

A Critic's Apology for Editing Dryden's *The History of the League*, by Alan Roper.

To Tell a Story: Narrative Theory and Practice. 1973.

Distributing the Middle: Problems of "Movement" in Narrative Poetry, by Earl Miner.

Mode in Narrative Poetry, by Paul Alpers.

Sequence and Meaning in Seventeenth-Century Narrative, by Stanley E. Fish.

Theory of the ΛΟΓΟΙ: The Speeches in Classical and Renaissance Narrative, by Richard A. Lanham.

Autobiography, Biography, and the Novel. 1973.

Seventeenth-Century Autobiography, by William Matthews.

Defoe, Richardson, Joyce, and the Concept of Form in the Novel, by Ralph W. Rader.

English Portraits of the Seventeenth and Eighteenth Centuries. 1974.

Pin-ups or Virtues: The Concept of the "Beauties" in Late Stuart Portraiture, by J. Douglas Stewart.

Portraits of the Author: Lifetime Likenesses of Samuel Johnson, by Herman W. Liebert.

Literature and History. 1974.

Innovation and Variation: Literary Change and Georgic Poetry, by Ralph Cohen.

Fiction and Historical Reality: The Hourglass and the Sands of Time, by Murray Krieger.

The English Legal System: Carryover to the Colonies. 1975.

The English Criminal Law in Early America, by Joseph H. Smith.

Law and Liberty (and Order) in Early Massachusetts, by Thomas G. Barnes.

Two English Novelists: Aphra Behn and Anthony Trollope. 1975.

Aphra Behn's *Oroonoko*: Occasion and Accomplishment, by George Guffey.

Anthony Trollope as a Reader, by Andrew Wright.

In Search of Restoration and Eighteenth-Century Theatrical Biography. 1976.

David Garrick and the Eighteenth-Century Stage, by George Winchester Stone, Jr.

A Peep behind the Curtain: Mass Theatrical Biography, by Philip H. Highfill, Jr.

Montana Past and Present. 1976.

They Drew from Power: An Introduction to Northern Cheyenne Ledger Book Art, by Father Peter J. Powell.

Montana as a Corporate Bailiwick: An Image in History, by Michael P. Malone.

Anglo-Dutch Cross Currents in the Seventeenth and Eighteenth Centuries. 1976.

The Last of the Renaissance Monsters: *The Poetical Institutions* of Gerardus Joannis Vossius, and Some Observations on English Criticism, by Paul R. Sellin.

The Myth of the Grand Alliance in the Eighteenth Century, by Stephen B. Baxter.

Hermeticism and the Scientific Revolution. 1977.

Magical Reform and Astronomical Reform: The Yates Thesis Reconsidered, by Robert S. Westman.

Neoplatonism and Active Principles: Newton and the *Corpus Hermeticum,* by J. E. McGuire.

Oscar Wilde: Two Approaches. 1977.

A Late Victorian Love Affair, by Richard Ellmann.

Resources for Wilde Studies at the Clark Library, by John Espey.

China and the West: Culture and Commerce. 1977.

Early China and the West: Fertilization and Fetalization, by Richard C. Rudolph.

America's Trade with Canton, by Schuyler Van Rensselaer Cammann.

Building Book Collections: Two Variations on a Theme. 1977.

Some Experiences of a Scholar-Collector, by James M. Osborn.

Books for Libraries: Institutional Book Collecting, by Robert Vosper.

The Colonial Printer: Two Views, by Robert D. Harlan. 1978.

Theories of History. 1978.

Rhetoric and History, by Hayden White.

The *Philosophes* in Doubt, by Frank E. Manuel.

John Dryden II. 1978.

Continuity and Coruscation: Dryden's Poetic Instincts, by Irvin

Ehrenpreis.
Dryden, Shadwell, and "a late fall'n Poet," by James M. Osborn.
The Renaissance Man in the Eighteenth Century. 1978.
Benjamin Franklin, Universal Genius, by J. A. Leo Lemay.
John Hill, Universal Genius *Manqué:* Remarks on His Life and Times, with a Checklist of His Works, by G. S. Rousseau.
English Scientific Virtuosi in the Sixteenth and Seventeenth Centuries. 1979.
History and Natural History in Sixteenth- and Seventeenth-Century England: An Essay on the Relationship between Humanism and Science, by Barbara Shapiro.
The Physician as Virtuoso in Seventeenth-Century England, by Robert G. Frank, Jr.
The American Southwest: Image and Reality. 1979.
The Image of the Southwest in Early European "Westerns," by Ray Allen Billington.
Historical Patterns in the Development of Chicano Urban Society: Southern California, 1848–1930, by Albert Camarillo.
John Locke. 1980.
The Myth of John Locke and the Obsession With Liberalism, by J. G. A. Pocock.
The *Two Treatises* and the Exclusion Crisis: The Problem of Lockean Political Theory as Bourgeois Ideology, by Richard Ashcraft.
English Hymnology in the Eighteenth Century. 1980.
The Language of the Eighteenth-Century Hymn, by Donald Davie.
The Eighteenth-Century Hymn Tune, by Robert Stevenson.

---

*These seminar papers have been collected in a volume edited by Earl Miner and published with the title: *Stuart and Georgian Moments: Clark Library Seminar Papers on Seventeenth and Eighteenth Century Literature* (University of California Press: $8.50).

The Press has also published five collections of essays presented, outside the seminar series, at the Clark Library:

England in the Restoration and Early Eighteenth Century: Essays on Culture and Society, edited by H. T. Swedenberg, Jr. ($12.00). Contributions by Robert M. Adams, Bertrand H. Bronson, Jean H. Hagstrum, James W. Johnson, John Loftis, Maximillian E. Novak, C. D. O'Malley, James M. Osborn, and Robert R. Wark.

Illustrious Evidence: Approaches to Early Seventeenth-Century Literature, edited by Earl Miner ($9.50). Contributions by Robert M. Adams, Stanley E. Fish, Frank L. Huntley, Barbara K. Lewalski, Louis L. Martz, and James Thorpe.

The Compleat Plattmaker: Essays on Chart, Map, and Globe Making in England in the Seventeenth and Eighteenth Centuries, edited by Norman J. W. Thrower ($14.95). Contributions by Jeannette D. Black, Thomas R. Smith, Norman J. W. Thrower, Coolie Verner, Helen M. Wallis, and David A. Woodward.

English Literature in the Age of Disguise, edited by Maximillian E. Novak ($12.95). Contributions by Ralph Cohen, Donald Greene, Maynard Mack, C. J. Rawson, Manuel Schonhorn, and John Traugott.

Culture and Politics from Puritanism to the Enlightenment, edited by Perez Zagorin ($14.95). Contributions by Robert M. Adams, Charles Gray, J. H. Hexter, Isaac Kramnick, Ronald Paulson, J. G. A. Pocock, Richard H. Popkin, John M. Wallace, Richard S. Westfall, and Perez Zagorin.

84